"Joe White is today's voice of wisdom for parents of teens. Great questions throughout this book are guaranteed to improve your communication with your teen."

—SUSAN ALEXANDER YATES, Bestselling author, *And Then I Had Teenagers* and *31 Days of Prayer for My Teen*

"Few people in my experience have more knowledge about—or love for—teens than Joe White. In *Sticking with Your Teen*, Joe draws from his years of experience as a father and as the operator of a highly successful youth camp to offer a wealth of practical insights to help parents manage the teen years with grace, peace, and understanding. If some expert 'teen advice' is what you need, you'll find it here."

—TOM FORTSON, PH.D., President and CEO, Promise Keepers

"Joe White is America's foremost expert in understanding the heartbeat of teens! Joe has championed the love and respect of countless parents and teens across America for decades—and we are two of his greatest fans! All of us as parents—from time to time and from child to child—want to understand why our teens become distant, and learn how to help them root out the issues. Hold on to your seatbelts, because *Sticking with Your Teen* delivers how to do it! Joe gives us a game plan that guarantees turning things around and potentially saving your relationship with your teen. It doesn't matter whether your child is wayward or winsome; it really is all about *you*. Read it and get the help you need to understand your teen!"

—DR. GARY AND BARBARA ROSBERG, America's Family Coaches

"An invaluable and inspiring resource for anyone parenting an adolescent. With a great sense of reality and understanding of today's teens plus many practical ideas for building relationship, this book will give readers hope and staying power to go the distance with their teen. I highly recommend it!"

—CHERI FULLER, Author, *When Teens Pray* and *The Mom You're Meant to Be: Loving Your Kids While Leaning on God*

"You're gonna love 'em—both Joe *and* this book! Honest. Potent. Straightforward. If you're mystified by your teenager, you'll love this little treasure store of wisdom. It's full of healthy conviction and powerful encouragement as well as solid hope and practical advice. You and your teen just may fall in love again."

—STU WEBER, Pastor and author

"An incredibly relevant and practical guide for parents trying to navigate through the tough years of raising teens. Joe White paints an accurate and sometimes even painful picture of the different scenarios moms and dads find themselves in—then offers insightful and real-world solutions. What I was most impressed with is how gut-level honestly and authentically Joe describes his own struggles and victories. This book will inspire and equip you to be a better parent to your teenager."

—Greg Stier, CEO, Dare 2 Share Ministries International

"Sticking with a distant or defiant teenager is one of the toughest assignments of parenthood. Joe White and Lissa Johnson don't spare the gory details—including the fact that you and I can be part of the problem. Fortunately, we can jumpstart the solution. This book is packed with powerful remedies that any dad or mom can carry out."

—STEVE FARRAR, Bestselling author, *Point Man* and *Finishing Strong*

STICKING WITH YOUR TEEN

FOCUS ON THE FAMILY
RESOURCES

STICKING
WITH YOUR TEEN

Joe White
with Lissa Halls Johnson

Tyndale House Publishers, Inc.
Carol Stream, Illinois

Library of Congress Cataloging-in-Publication Data

White, Joe, 1948—
    Sticking with your teen: how to keep from coming unglued no matter what / Joe White
with Lissa Halls Johnson.
        p. cm.
    "Focus on the Family."
    Includes bibliographical references (p.).
    1. Child rearing—Religious aspects—Christianity. 2. Parent and teenager—Religious
aspects—Christianity. 3. Problem children. I. Johnson, Lissa Halls, 1955— II. Title.
    BV4529.W544 2005
    248.8'45—dc22

                                                                              2005025109

ISBN 10: 1-58997-315-1
ISBN 13: 978-1-58997-315-2

Contents

A Word from Joe

There are no magic pills or potions that make us great parents, and no magic deeds that guarantee our efforts will "work."

Great parents can have prodigal children.

Horrible parents can have great children.

Some parents have kids on both ends of the spectrum—same environment, different outcomes.

No matter which kind of teen you have, chances are that sometimes you've wanted to wring his neck. You may get so frustrated at his stubbornness that you want to scream, and sometimes do. Well, join the rest of us.

But there's hope. I realized this recently when I danced with my daughter at her wedding. Reaching out her slender hand, she led me to the dance floor. Tears flowed as I cherished every moment, every memory of our years together.

Things had not always been good between my daughter and me. For too many years they were hard, so hard. As I let my tears fall, I knew this was the crowning moment.

I want this for you as well. It's the payoff for all your hard work—dancing with your daughter at her wedding, standing up for your son at his, being asked by your adult son to help him with his first business venture.

Think it's impossible? Well, look at me. I'm a dad who started out much too busy. But by the grace of God, my daughter and I danced at her wedding, and only the best of our memories remained.

"It Was Worth It"

The chaos of having four teens in the house is as distant in my memory as a sliver of new moon on a foggy January night. But the good times seem like yesterday.

I don't miss the long, sleepless nights, but how I miss the adolescents who caused them! I don't miss the conflicts, but I miss the precious ones with whom I shared them. I don't miss the seemingly hopeless sea of misunderstanding, but I miss the waves of hope that flowed to the shore when reconciliation came.

Now the phone rings with calls from my precious grandchildren. I'm discovering the wisdom of the old gentleman who said, "If I'd known being a granddad was this much fun, I would have been a whole lot nicer to my kids!"

Dancing in the firelight that flickers with memories is good at age 56. The leukemia that five years ago threatened to kill me is now in remission; my teenagers are in their twenties, at peace with their mom and dad and raising children of their own.

I can honestly say, "It was worth it a billion times over; it was worth it!" The seasons of rebellion and rejection pale in comparison to the smiles and gratitude and accomplishments and team-building and spiritual growth that crowd the treasure chest of my memories.

Not that everything is perfect. My kids still catch me in "hopeless Dad" mode. The other day I was hustling from my car to the front door of the mall, talking to my oldest son. It dawned on me that I must have left my cell phone in my car. I went back and looked everywhere, but without success.

"I think I lost my phone," I told my son.

"Dad," he laughed in pity, "you're *talking* to me on your phone!"

Maybe it's God's design that our memory gets a little "selective" at my age. It seems all the days I made "D's" and "F's" as a frustrated dad are, like my cell phone, lost to my conscious mind.

You Make the Difference

Your home life, like mine, may not be pretty all the time. Our parenting may not be perfect. Our teens may seem standoffish or downright mutinous.

But we moms and dads can make the difference. We can stand firmly at home plate, swinging at the fastballs and curveballs that parenting teens hurls in our direction. Our hugs may not always seem appreciated, but we can deal them out knowing that someday, someone will be nurtured by them.

Our "I love yous" and "I'm proud of yous" may seem like sparse raindrops on the desert of our teens' hearts, but at least they're hearing them. The day may well dawn when the phone rings and the long-awaited words flow humbly through the earpiece: "Thanks, Mom. Thanks, Dad. You are the best! You never quit on me. Even when I didn't love myself, you did. Even when I didn't know how to receive love, you gave it. Even when everyone else abandoned me, you always stood in my corner."

I Hope You Dance

Dancing may be the activity furthest from your mind right now. Maybe screaming or sobbing or throwing a brick through a window would express your emotions more clearly. Maybe it seems your teen is so far away, or so sunk in trouble, that reconnecting is impossible.

But if I've learned anything from parenting teens and from talking with tens of thousands of them at Kanakuk Kamps and elsewhere, it's this: *It's never too late to start, and it's always too soon to quit!*

The western Kansas farmer never stops planting milo, corn, and wheat in his faith-filled springtime ritual. Drought after drought, disappointing harvest after disappointing harvest, he never stops believing, never stops hoping, never stops casting seed into the parched ground. Somewhere in his heart there's a dream of a vibrant sea of early August five-foot stalks, filled with golden ears of corn awaiting the blade of the combine.

The soil of your teen's heart may seem hard right now. But the plow and the rains are on the way, and the harvest is coming.

This is a book about believing in that day, and in the God who's going to help you and your teen get there together.

A Word from Lissa

I'm scared of heights. So why was I three stories up, my legs dangling over nothing?

I knew others had made it safely down this 300-foot zip line at Kamp Kanakuk, speeding at treetop level to a brick stop at the other end. Some had even done it upside-down.

I knew it *could* be done safely. But would *my* ride be safe?

There was no more time to contemplate. The person running the ride began the countdown and shouted, "Geronimo!" I threw myself off the bench and flew down the line—screaming the entire way.

At the other end, my six companion zippers asked if I'd had fun. I said, "I don't know. I was too scared to tell."

I think many parents of teenagers feel the same way.

They're scared before raising their teens, and they're scared during. Afterward, they have no idea if they did it right—or if they had fun doing it.

Time to Reconnect

For some parents, the process is especially frightening. The sweet child who threw chubby arms around their necks and said, "I wub you, Mommy, Daddy," now gives them an obscene gesture. These parents may have done their best to raise that teen in a godly, loving way. But something genetic, tragic, mistaken, or mysterious causes their child to snap.

For other parents, it's not so dramatic. They just wake up one morning and realize they're living with a stranger. Or at least someone who seems not to need them anymore.

We all have days like that. We flounder, wondering how to connect with our teens. Should we even try? Is it too late?

Some of us give up. Others try to exert more control.

Neither approach works.

We're here to encourage you to climb back up the spiral staircase to the zip-line platform. We'll strap you into the harness and make you as secure as we can. But at the count of three, you'll have to push yourself off the bench and begin your wild descent.

We don't offer recipes to "fix" your teen. We do offer an arm around the shoulder as you learn to become a relentless parent—one who never, ever gives up.

We've been down that zip line ourselves. Our own kids have acted out their anger and frustration over hurts we caused and some we didn't. We did the best we could and made some mistakes—and discoveries—along the way.

We'd like to share the most helpful parts with you.

Relational and Relentless

This book is about reengaging a disengaged teen. It contains no easy answers, no steps that guarantee success. That's because every human being has the right to choose wisdom or stupidity. You can guide and encourage your teen, but you can't choose for him.

Fortunately, that guidance and encouragement can make all

the difference in the world. They did for a boy I met at Kamp Kanakuk. His father, an all-American football hero, had dreams for his son to follow in his footsteps—and the son shared that dream. The two of them trained long and hard until a doctor discovered that the boy had a congenital back problem that made it unwise for him to play football. Just like that, the dream was gone.

What did that father do? He threw his arms around the boy and said, "It doesn't matter, son. We'll have a new dream. I know you can do anything you set your mind to do, and you will."

When I met him, that boy barely could sit still; he was that excited. "I can do anything," he exclaimed, "because my dad believes in me."

Connecting with your teen requires that kind of belief. It requires not giving up. It requires letting your teen make mistakes and then beginning again.

It's the kind of thing God has done for us. He's allowed us to choose a relationship with Him—or not. Every day we have that choice.

That's what we're going to do in this book—learn who we need to be so that our teens have every opportunity and reason to choose a relationship with us.

It's never too late to start that process.

And it's always too soon to quit.

You may not be sure right now whether the zip line of parenting a teen is worth the effort—or the risk. By the time you finish this book, though, I hope the how *and* the why will be clear.

It's about being relational—and relentless.

And when you get to the other end, it's about breathing a sigh of relief—and recognizing that, in spite of everything, there really were some good times after all.

1

The Experiment

*My mom and I do not get along very well, so we usually
find ourselves disputing over the simplest things. Lately she
has been very judgmental of my friends because of their
hair or the way that they dress. She brings up the old cliché
line, "Name someone successful that looks like that," and
I always come back with, "We're teenagers. We're not
supposed to be successful; it's our experimental years."*

—A TEEN

If the teen years are experimental, how's the experiment going at
your house? Are you on the verge of a great discovery? Or are you
afraid to enter the lab each morning for fear of the rotten-egg
smell and the mold growing in the corner? Or are you ready to
hang a DANGER sign on the wall?

Sandra and Richard McDonald found themselves in the danger category at two o'clock one morning.

When the doorbell rang, Sandra dragged herself from a deep
sleep. Her husband, Richard, rolled out of bed.

At the front door, Richard was surprised to see Ken Bell, an
acquaintance of his own son, Kurt. Ken's father was there, too.

"Mr. Bell?" Richard said.

The man nodded. "Ken's truck was broken into. They smashed the windows. Stole the stereo." He cleared his throat, looking uneasy. "Ken says he saw your son's truck leaving the scene."

Sandra felt her heart race. "Someone must have stolen Kurt's truck."

"Kurt is spending the night with a friend," Richard told the Bells. "We'll find out what happened and get back to you."

After the men left, Sandra called her son's cell phone. "Kurt!" she said.

"Mom, why are you calling so late?"

"Where's your truck?"

"I don't know. Outside, I guess. Why?"

"Well, you're not going to believe this, but Mr. Bell and Ken came by. Ken's truck was broken into. Your truck was leaving the area. Look outside; is your truck outside?"

Kurt made some noises, then said, "No, it's gone."

"I'm going to get him," Richard told Sandra.

> "You're looking at [your teen] and you're thinking, yeah, he is a little less communicative, but it seems like everything's okay."
>
> —A PARENT

Soon Richard and Kurt were driving around town, looking for Kurt's truck. But Kurt was calm—pretty strange, Richard thought, considering the boy's truck supposedly was stolen.

As they drove, Kurt began to talk. Puzzle pieces fell from nowhere. He admitted that he'd been hanging out with a kid, Jeremy, who everyone knew was bad news.

This shock had barely landed when Kurt added, "Oh, yeah, Dad—I'm moving to Mexico with Jeremy."

Dumbfounded, Richard barely managed to keep steering the car.

"We're leaving as soon as Jeremy gets this huge inheritance when he turns 18."

More silence.

"It's all planned."

The puzzle pieces fell into place, creating a picture Richard didn't want to see. Instead of asking about the planned move, though, he probed the whereabouts of the truck.

Kurt's answer gave him another jolt: "Well, I can't remember anything, because I took Xanax and I've been drinking." The boy fidgeted. "Well, yeah, maybe I was there. Maybe I did help Jeremy break into that car. And maybe, you know, maybe, that stuff we stole out of the other car is kind of . . . well . . . actually in my truck. Jeremy is kind of, well, driving it."

Overwhelmed, Richard pulled the car to the side of the road. He sat there with the car running, staring at his son. "What else?"

"Well, I guess—yeah, I guess the cops are chasing him right now."

Is that how the experiment is going at your house?

Maybe the developments in your "lab" aren't quite so dramatic, but they're just as frustrating. Maybe conversations with your teen go something like this:

"Jen! How was school?"

Glare. "Fine."

"Did you do anything fun?"

Glare. "No."

"How was your math test?"

Glare. "Stupid."

"Come sit and talk to me."

"Why should I?"

"I'd just like to know—"

"I've got homework." Footsteps pound up the stairs. A door slams.

Or maybe you're hearing more silence than sarcasm these days:

"Hi, Scott. How was your day?"

Grunt.

Backpack drops to the floor. Footsteps fade down the hall.

Sound familiar?

Whether your teen-raising experiment is going terribly wrong or not, chances are it isn't quite meeting your expectations. You may feel like the child you knew has switched places with a taller, gangly person you couldn't possibly have given birth to.

> "We didn't want to continue down the path we were on, but we didn't want to give up on having a relationship with her."
> —A PARENT

Well, come on in and join me. I've lived through that experiment.

My wife, Debbie Jo, and I had four teens in the house at the same time. What a ride those years were! I wish I could tell you I did everything right, but I didn't. We had broken curfews, defiant attitudes, intense sibling rivalry, late-night phone calls that revealed things I never wanted to hear, emotional meltdowns, the silent treatment, depression, rejection, and rebellion. The season on any behavior, with any kid, could last a day, a month, and sometimes years. Many times I'd wake up in the morning and think, *What in the world is going on?*

Depending on how your experiment is going, you may feel sometimes like you're on the verge of a nervous breakdown. You may be going bald from all that head-scratching and hair-pulling.

You're probably trying the best you can. But you've noticed the relationship with your son or daughter is getting distant—or downright fractured. You want to be connected with your teen, to continue to help shape his life, but something's happened. You may not be sure what to do. And even if you are, you wonder whether it's too late.

Confessions of a Former Teenager

Before you can figure out what to do about your situation, you need to decide just how bad things really are. One way to do that is to remember what things were like when *you* were a teen.

Let's take a little trip down memory lane, shall we?

Remember those raging hormones? Maybe you resisted the urges they created; maybe you didn't.

Remember how you saw your parents? Maybe you listened to them; maybe you preferred your friends' ideas. Slowly or quickly you moved away from your folks, trying to become your own person.

Remember your relationships with other kids? You wanted to be noticed, to be loved, to find a circle of friends where you fit in.

And those industrial-strength feelings—remember them? Sometimes you felt angry for no apparent reason. If you were a girl, maybe you felt like crying all the time. If you were a boy, maybe you wanted to punch something every couple of hours. The smallest event could throw you into one mood or another, or several at once.

Did you rebel as a teen, or just disconnect a little? Maybe you bought clothes your parents would never buy, listened to music they hated. Or maybe you went off the deeper end, skipping school or binge drinking or dealing grass or rolling an SUV at 90 miles per hour and ending your best friend's life.

Times Have Changed

Recalling your teenaged self can help put your son's or daughter's behavior in perspective, especially if you were a headache-producing handful. But if you were no more rebellious than Beaver Cleaver, you may ask, "Why can't my kid be more like I was?"

Part of the answer may lie in the fact that Beaver's world is long gone. The emotions and questions of adolescence may be the same, but practically everything else has changed. Friendships can be established and built on the Internet, without face-to-face contact. Knowledge—good, bad, and perverted—is on tap there, too. Kids stay in touch on personal phones that go with them everywhere. Thousands of songs in a tiny metal box provide a soundtrack for their lives.

> "You were a kid once, too. Be sure your kids understand that."
>
> —A PARENT

Think the world hasn't changed all that much? I heard recently of a young actress who needed to play a scene in a movie that showed her putting a record on a turntable. She had to be taught how to do it; she'd never even *seen* a record!

The most important changes, though, aren't technological—they're moral. Everything from radio deejay talk to comic books is far more graphic than it was two decades ago. Drugs and alcohol are more accessible and acceptable, even in many Christian circles. Premarital sex is more expected than shameful; "hooking up" is a way for casual friends to experience anything from kissing to oral sex to intercourse. One girl told her mother, "Mom, Daniel and I are the only kids in my school *and* church that I know who are not sexually involved."

Our teens today live in a world of hurt. They're hurt by broken homes and broken promises. They're victimized by sexual abuse, date rape, gang violence, and bullying. They're growing up in the shadow of threats most of us didn't face—like terrorism and school shootings. If they're trying too hard to control their world, the results may not be excusable—just understandable.

> *"When you have a child that is basically dominating the entire family life—that's what they do, they take over the whole [family]—they're the center of attention all the time, 24/7. The other two kids get shoved under the rug."*
>
> —A PARENT

Warning Signs

So, have you seen hints that trouble is brewing in your "lab"? Is your teen distant? Belligerent? Is the relationship you'd hoped for disappearing under indifference, anger, or defiance?

Sometimes the signs couldn't be clearer. "[Our son] David took a ball off the pool table and threw it at my husband, who ducked," recalls one mom. "It broke a window, and David picked up a chair and threw it down the hall, broke a leg off the chair. . . . So my sister, my husband and I spent the night locked in our bedroom. That's where we all three slept that night, in the bedroom, locked up."

Another parent remembers: "[Our daughter] hauled off and threw a glass of Coke or something at my face—and I really did think for a second that I was going to kill her. I was just ready to annihilate her. I was embarrassed and so outraged that I thought, 'I'm going to kill you.'"

"Pretty much from day one, we knew [our son] was going to be a challenge. . . . We never were able to really break that independent, strong spirit that was so defiant."

—A PARENT

Still another parent recalls, "Sometimes [our son] Kyle would say, 'I would rather go to juvenile hall than live with you all.'"

Maybe the hints have arrived more quietly. You may have found a marijuana bag, or a pack of condoms, or the empty aerosol cans and rags and paper sacks that indicate "huffing."

Or maybe you're worried about smaller earthquakes. Your daughter paints her fingernails black. Your son gets his nose pierced. You hear "I hate you!" more than any other phrase—or you hardly hear anything at all.

Try taking a quick test to figure out whether there might be a problem at your place. Do you identify with any of the following statements?

____ I don't like my teen.

____ My teen doesn't like me.

____ I'm embarrassed for anyone to know what my family life is really like.

____ I don't want anyone to know what my kid is doing.

____ I don't like my teen's choices.

____ I want to fix my teen.

If you find yourself agreeing with any of those statements, chances are that your relationship with your teen is stretched, strained, or snapped.

Welcome to the club.

You're Not the Boss of Me

Admitting things aren't going well is scary. It means you have to do something.

So what can you do about this?

A lot of parents, especially Christian ones, try the "crack-down." Determined to make their teens submit to authority, they haul out the howitzers—rules on stone tablets, year-long ground-ings, sermonettes, house arrest.

The problem is that these parents don't realize their job description has changed since their kids were little. Teens need parents who have moved from governor to mentor, from commander to coach, from benevolent dictator to guide. It's time to be an advisor, not a puppet master.

> "Every time we tried to talk ended up being constant yelling back and forth in the house. It would get so bad sometimes that my sister would run next door to my aunt's house."
> —A TEEN

It's hard to make that transition.

When my kids started "breaking away," they just about broke my fingers trying to peel away my grip of steel. I wanted so badly to protect them. When they told me how rough the language was on the school bus, and about the bully that picked on them, I wanted to ride with them or drive them to school or walk them to class. But I couldn't. When they started dating, I wanted to dou-ble-date so I could keep them out of trouble. But I couldn't.

The trick, I learned, is allowing the transition to happen gradu-ally. Start off firm, slowly giving way to more liberty. If you come in with handcuffs, you'll become a controlling, frustrated parent with a rebellious teen.

Some parents wouldn't think of trying the crackdown. They're more likely to give up. *It's out of my hands*, they think. *I've done all I can. She'll be leaving home soon. And she won't listen to me anyway.*

> "Our oldest son's life philosophy is, 'No problem.' Our younger son's life philosophy would come down to, 'Says who?'"
>
> —A PARENT

The truth is that our kids need us more than ever when they're teens. Not as controllers, but as counselors.

"Hey," you may be saying. "I'm no counselor. I don't even understand why my kid is acting this way."

You're not alone.

So let's look at that in the next chapter.

Let's find out why your teen may be growing distant or self-destructive. Let's put that young person under the microscope—or at least the magnifying glass.

Sounds pretty scientific, doesn't it?

But that's okay.

Like I said, this is an experiment. Before you know it, you'll be breaking out the test tubes—and improving the chemistry between you and your teen.

2

What's Wrong with That Kid?

But [with our daughter] . . . it was always, "I'm going to ride my bike around the block because you told me not to. And I'm going to be the one in charge." That's a hard way to go through life, because you're missing out on the experience of all these people around you who know that you walk down that road and it's dangerous.

—A PARENT

She's . . . really never respected authority. She is her own authority. She has always placed herself on an equal basis with adults starting at about age 10. She's "right" and she's very argumentative.

—ANOTHER PARENT

His attitude started changing. He just started being kind of more and more of a bully with his younger brother. He started stealing. He had failed every class. There wasn't any twinkle in his eye anymore at all.

—STILL ANOTHER PARENT

Which of the following apply to you?

1. ___ Your is teen respectful and responsible most of the time.

2. ____ Your teen has faults, but you suspect she's reacting to (or imitating) your own.

3. ____ You get feedback from others about what a "great kid you have," even if you don't see it at home.

4. ____ Your teen may not always respond the way you'd like, but generally chooses friends well, does homework (if grudgingly), and can be coerced into doing chores.

5. ____ Your teen seems to respond well to you when things are calm at home.

6. ____ Your teen's behavior hasn't changed radically and negatively in the last year.

7. ____ Your teen seems to get angry at nothing, blowing up at the slightest provocation.

8. ____ Your teen is defiant no matter what you say or do.

9. ____ Your teen seems to be saying or doing things continually to hurt you or to prove you have no control over him.

10. ____ Your teen consistently walks in grumpy and leaves grumpy no matter what you say or do.

11. ____ Your teen never communicates; all your attempts at even casual conversation are thwarted.

12. ____ Your teen is involved in drugs, sexual promiscuity, or alcohol abuse.

> "He certainly wasn't willing to behave or conform to any norms that existed in our household."
> —A PARENT

If you chose one or more of statements 1-6, chances are that your teen's behavior falls into the "normal range" for today's adolescents. There may be distance, but there's hope.

If you chose one or more of statements 7-12, you face more of a challenge. Distance may have turned to hostility, even self-destruction.

You may need outside help to turn things around—but there's hope for you, too.

Either way, a first step toward success is understanding why things have changed in your relationship with your son or daughter. Is it all hormones and peer pressure?

Sure, those factors often play a role. But many parents miss the events—big or little—that can knock a teen off course. You might call them "trigger points."

Pulling the Trigger

I've talked with an army of moms and dads whose teens' problems seemed to begin with a specific event. "Up until that time he'd been a model child," one parent—like so many others—said.

Sometimes the triggers don't look traumatic:

"Our trouble began when she started driving her car."

"Yeah, I mean she's a good mom," said one boy. "It's just that when I started to change my opinions on stuff and change what I

> "Apparently they were much more intense anxieties than we knew. And so he would medicate those. Performance anxieties, school, peer pressure, things normally kids don't escalate. From our perspective he didn't look like he was full of anxiety. To me he looked confident; he always had friends around, he was always invited to go places, he made good grades—he's very popular. He's funny. People really like him."
>
> —A PARENT

do, she hasn't been real accepting about it. It's made it hard for me. She wants me to think the way she does. I'd just like her to accept my opinions."

Some triggers may be more obvious to observers, but not to the parents involved. One parent declared, "Even though I was there for him, [my son thought] that somehow I wasn't there for him because I had married and I had these other responsibilities."

Sometimes the triggers are delayed, even by years. "We adopted him when he was one week old. We never dreamed that he would feel the rejection that apparently he felt."

> "What in the world did we do? How could this have happened to us? Because where did we screw up? We look back and we just can't find it, can't see it. I know we didn't do well. I mean we weren't perfect parents, but I know a lot of people that do a worse job and their kids are going to Princeton."
>
> —A PARENT

Other triggers are more "in your face." "I moved 18 times in my life," recalled one troubled teen. Another said, "My stepfather was verbally, emotionally, physically, and sexually abusive to me and so I never felt I could tell anyone, not even my mom. . . . I got so caught up in so much anger and hate towards him that I just started trying to find ways out. Like, an example was I started drinking and doing some things I should not have been doing."

When a teen's world turns upside-down—or just tilts slightly on its axis—she may hunt for stability by seeking your attention and acceptance. If the attention isn't forthcoming, she may create chaos in order to be noticed. If the acceptance doesn't flow, she may try to get it from peers—sometimes at a terrible price.

You can't shield your teen from traumas. But you can do your best to notice them. You can gauge how your teen is reacting to them. And you can resist society's claim that "flexible" children will take disruptions like divorce and remarriage in stride.

Your Teen's Triggers

Think about what's happened to your teen during the last year. Is it possible that any of those events might have sparked strong emotions in him? Could it be that he doesn't know how to talk to you about those feelings?

Check the following list for situations that may have triggered alienation or rebellion.

1. ___ Your teen didn't make the team, band, play cast, club, or other group he'd planned for, hoped for, or trained for.
2. ___ Your teen loves someone who doesn't return the affection.
3. ___ Your teen has no date to a big event like homecoming or prom.
4. ___ Your teen broke up with a boyfriend or girlfriend (even if your teen initiated it).
5. ___ Your teen has been sitting on the bench for too many games.
6. ___ Your teen is bullied or teased frequently.
7. ___ Your teen has teacher trouble.
8. ___ Your teen is doing poorly in school.
9. ___ Your teen has suddenly gained weight.
10. ___ Your teen has changed schools.
11. ___ Your teen has been embarrassed in front of friends.

12. ____ Your teen is at odds with a best friend or group of friends.
13. ____ Something has been stolen from your teen.
14. ____ Your family moved recently.
15. ____ A grandparent, sibling, or other person has moved into the family home.
16. ____ There's been a divorce or separation in your family.
17 ____ A parent has abandoned the family.
18. ____ You've remarried.
19. ____ You're dating.
20. ____ A friend, family member, schoolmate, or pet has died.
21. ____ A friend or family member has been seriously ill or injured.
22. ____ Your teen has been the victim of rape or date rape.
23. ____ Your teen has been sexually abused.
24. ____ Your teen has been physically abused.
25. ____ Your teen has discovered that one of his parents is involved with drugs, alcohol, violence, or pornography.
26. ____ There is conflict between you and your mate, or between a parent and another child.
27. ____ Your teen's sibling (especially an older one) is in trouble, has experienced a tragedy, or has gone away to college.
28. ____ Your teen's close friend has experienced any of these events.
29. ____ Your teen has discovered a moral failure in someone she trusted or respected.

30. ____ Your teen has been reminded by a traumatic world event (9/11, the tsunami of 2004, etc.) that he is not in control of life.

This list isn't exhaustive, of course. And don't forget that even positive events can lead to troublesome behavior. For example, has your teen gotten a driver's license or learner's permit? Purchased a car? Moved from middle school to high school? Gained a boyfriend or girlfriend?

Getting Some Answers

Checklists can take you only so far. If you really want to know why your teen acts the way he does, ask him! It's worth a try.

I'll have more to say about communication in Chapter 7, but for now let me show you a tried and true method I use to get kids talking about what's bothering them. It's called active listening.

Begin by asking, "Would you like to talk about it now?"

If the answer is no, try again later.

When your teen is open to talking, ask, "What's wrong?"

Listen to the answer. Then ask, "How do you feel?"

> "My kid is one of those guys who's determined to learn all of life's lessons the hard way."
> —A PARENT

Listen some more. Then ask, "What are you doing about it?"

Listen again. Then ask, "What do you need to do?"

Listen further. Keep cycling through the questions as needed.

Let's see how this works in real life.

Your daughter comes home, sighs, drops her backpack on the floor, and slumps onto the couch.

"Do you feel like talking about it?" you ask.

"I guess," the girl mumbles.

"What's wrong?"

"Kerry told Shannon that I copied her test."

"How do you feel?"

"I'm totally angry at Kerry. She knows it's a lie. She knows I don't cheat."

"What are you doing about it?

"I don't know."

"What do you need to do?"

Your daughter shrugs and stares at the floor.

"What's wrong?" you ask again.

"I don't know if Kerry is my friend. I don't know why she'd say that."

"How do you feel about that?"

"Confused. Hurt."

"What are you doing about it?"

"I told Kaitlyn and Jo and Susan at lunch."

"What do you *need* to do?"

Your daughter sighs. "I probably need to talk to Kerry. I don't want to, though. I don't know what to say to her."

"How do you feel about confronting her?"

"Scared."

You get the idea. In a conversation like that, your teen can let you in on the large and small traumas of her life, defusing their destructive power. It helps to have those exchanges as soon after the event as possible, but don't pressure your teen to talk. And if you've avoided those conversations for so long that it seems awkward to bring up "old business," remember: "Better late than never."

What Now?

If a life event has triggered distance or rebellion in your teen, talk with him about it. If that's beyond your skill, understanding, or patience, don't hesitate to find a counselor who specializes in teens—and in the kind of event (loss, abuse, divorce) your teen has undergone. A good therapist can help your whole family walk through this together.

If your teen refuses counseling, go by yourself. Find out how to handle your feelings, and how you can help your son or daughter.

Whether you deal with your teen's triggers on your own or with a counselor's aid, though, that's not the end of the story.

In fact, most of this story isn't about your teen. It's about *you*.

"Now, hold on," you may be saying. "Now that I understand my teen a little better, I can get him to clean up his act, right?"

Nope.

You may learn to understand your teen, but you can't "fix" him. You can't change *anybody*. You can only start to change yourself.

"What I've learned is, [our teen's behavior] is what it is and God, the great I Am, has allowed it to be what it is. And He has given her the DNA and the genes and everything that made her what she is. . . . All the good things she does, you know, I can't take credit for . . . and all the bad things, I don't have to take the blame for."
—A PARENT

In the next chapter you'll consider where those changes might begin. You'll have a chance to take a snapshot of how you're doing as a parent. The process may be a bit uncomfortable. But it's nothing compared with the pain of losing touch with your teen—and the joy of getting him back.

3

It's Never Too Late to Start . . . on Yourself

My relationship with my mom has been rough lately because all that she seems to care about are my grades and performance in school. She tries to monitor everything she can so that whenever I "drop the ball," she can get on me for it. She just needs to trust me and know that I can manage my own time and work, because if I don't learn to now, I may not be able to when I need to.

—A TEEN

Brent is a great kid. He's articulate, smart, generous. His parents raised him carefully, taking Brent and his siblings to church every Sunday. Dad worked long hours, but made sure he was home in the evening when the kids would need him. He'd go back to the office when they went to bed.

But something went wrong.

Behind the closed doors of Brent's home, all was not as it seemed. You sense that when you talk to Brent and his parents—separately. The stories are similar, but Brent tells of family patterns that show Mom and Dad missed something. For instance, Brent recalls, "My whole life [my father] just completely watched what I ate. He was a little chunky kid, I guess, and he didn't want me to get fat. Every time I ate something he was always watching me. So, it was a lot of pressure on me to fit what he wanted."

Had Brent's parents behaved differently, they might have avoided a ton of family heartbreak.

When the Truth Hurts

Am I trashing Brent's mom and dad?

Am I pointing a finger at you?

No. The fact is that I've been in their shoes, and yours. As a parent I've struggled, strained, fought, made mistakes, chosen wisely and foolishly, failed and succeeded.

I know the problems you're having with your teen may not be your fault. But if you want to get to the root of why your teen is tough to handle or be around, you have to be brutally honest with yourself. It's time for a clear-eyed look at what's going on in your home.

Are You Up for This?

Any Olympian will tell you that training is hard. It takes over your life, dictating what you eat, when you sleep, what you do each day. If I wanted to be a champion wrestler, I'd have to take a good look at my schedule and cut out everything that didn't lead to my goal. I wouldn't be able to do one of my favorite things—sitting in the Kamp Kanakuk dining hall with a heaping bowl of vanilla ice cream with lots of chocolate syrup, nuts, and sprinkles, talking to kids. I'd have to replace that ice cream with carrots or high-carb muscle fuel. Training isn't fun.

I'd like to be your trainer in this chapter. If I seem ruthless, it's because we're going for a great goal—to be gold-medal parents to our teens. We'll have to cut the ice cream and get to the truth.

Why Me?

Maybe you're wondering why you should give me a chance to be your trainer. That's a good question. I certainly don't have anything to boast about (2 Corinthians 12:5). But eating ice cream isn't the only thing I do at Kamp Kanakuk.

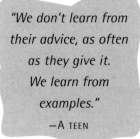

"We don't learn from their advice, as often as they give it. We learn from examples."

—A TEEN

I've had the privilege of counseling thousands of teens and parents during the last 30 years as they've come through our Kamps. Kids come to me with everything— unwanted pregnancies, porn addictions, suicide attempts. I feel their pain and cry with them. I pray with them. We talk about the resources God has given them, and how to find solutions they can live with.

The talking doesn't end when Kamp closes for the winter, either. Just the other day I had a call from a man who was on his way to rescue his 15-year-old niece. She's pregnant and tried twice to kill herself. We'll be talking a lot in the coming months as I share some things God has taught me.

That's all I want to do as your trainer. As a dad who's made many mistakes along the way, I'd like to help you shine the spotlight on your parenting—just as I've had to do on my own.

The Secret Lives of Families

When trouble appears in the form of a rebellious teen, many parents hide from the truth. It's not that they're lying; they just "forget" some important details.

I remember one set of parents whose teen daughter had been disruptive. In the middle of our conversation Mom and Dad dropped a bombshell: The girl had been raped. Then they just kept going. No wonder the young woman was having problems! She'd experienced a major, life-changing event—and her parents treated it as though it were a hangnail. Any teenage girl who'd gone through that could be expected to "act out" because she didn't know how to express her feelings otherwise.

Another pair of Christian parents seemed unaware that they were destroying one of their daughters by verbally abusing her.

"You're too fat," they'd tell her one day.

"You're too skinny," they'd tell her the next.

Then it was, "You're so stupid you'll never be a success at what you want to do."

When it became clear that the girl had become suicidal, the parents claimed to be mystified. Opening wide, innocent eyes, they told their friends at church, "We have no idea what's wrong with her. She's just moody."

Behind the doors of other Christian homes, other awful secrets have been kept. One girl opted out of "being good" when her pastor father was arrested for drug possession and use. Another slid downhill when her stepfather abused her. A young man couldn't deal with his father's pornography habit. And no one on the outside had any idea what was happening.

You may honestly say, "There's none of that going on in our

home." Thankfully, those are the exceptions. But do any of these scenes sound more familiar?

- Dad can't deliver a word of kindness without a qualifier: "You're a good-looking boy, but . . . " "You're a smart girl, but . . ."
- Mom and Dad go ballistic when their teen's hairstyle, T-shirt, or body piercing embarrasses them at church. They're sending a clear message to that son or daughter: "It's important to keep up our image, not for you to be a real person." The teen responds by vowing to show everyone just how "imperfect" he is.
- Stressed by her day job, Mom secludes herself in the bedroom watching "reality TV" every evening. Dad, afraid of being "downsized," glues his eyes to the Internet. Their teen locks himself in his room, shooting aliens online with strangers.

Can you open up your doors and let the truth step out? You might want to pray about that before reading the rest of this chapter. Ask God to show you the truth and set you free (John 8:32). Like training, truth often hurts—but it's the only way to the winner's circle.

Focus on Your Child's Parent

There's a problem in your house. Like the smell of dirty socks, it seems to drift from the area where your teen hangs out. Things are calm when she's not around; things are not calm when she's there.

So the problem must be with your teen, right?

Not necessarily.

But does it *matter* whose fault it is?

It only matters if there's something *you* can do about it. You can't change someone else, especially a teenager who's fighting himself and the rest of the world to become his own person. The only one you can change is yourself.

Are you willing to start there?

Many parents aren't. Counselors often see moms and dads who come in pointing their fingers at the teen: "Please fix her. She's the problem in our family."

Problems aren't that simple. And finger-pointing usually doesn't accomplish much. Neither does mimicking your teen in the middle of an argument when he yells or snorts or rolls his eyes. You're the adult here!

It's tempting to think, *If I could just change his attitude . . .*

Forget it.

Each person on this earth, including your teen, has a free will. God designed us this way. We can influence each other, but each person chooses to respond to that influence or not. The best way to influence your teen to change his attitude is by changing yours. Accepting responsibility for your own contributions to the situation might even help your teen to acknowledge her own.

What Kind of Parent Are You?

Okay, let's begin that frank assessment of how you're doing. This will only hurt for a while.

To start, take this little quiz.

With your teen, are you usually . . .

Demanding or polite?

Evasive or maintaining eye contact?

Whiny or confident?

Absent or present?

Distant or available?

Controlling or freeing?

Harsh or gentle?

Condescending or respectful?

Preoccupied or attentive?

Talking or listening?

Given each of those choices, which would you *like* to be?

Now let's play "20 Questions." If it helps to write your answers in a notebook or journal, feel free.

1. *Are you a reactive parent or a responsive one?*

If your teen comes home late from a party she didn't know would include drinking, do you start accusing and tossing out punishments like confetti? Or do you talk it through, asking questions and seeking to understand?

2. *Do you assume that when you assign something to your teen it will be done, not taking into account his homework schedule or other current events in his life?*

If your teen usually does the dishes on Wednesday nights, but this time has a huge Civics report due tomorrow, can you muster the grace to allow an exception?

3. *Do you relate to all members of the household without favoritism?*

Do you shout at one child but speak softly to another? Do you smile at one and frown at the other?

4. *Would you speak to your friends the way you speak to your teen?*

Would you *order* your friend to clean her room? Would you sigh in disgust if your friend couldn't figure out how to calculate the area of a circle?

5. *When you're frustrated with your teen, do you consider your options?*

Does that forgotten textbook or lost student ID card lead you to lash out, or do you take a break and say, "Sara, I'm really frustrated. If I try to deal with this now, I'm liable to yell at you and I don't want to do that. Let's take a break"?

6. *How often do you tell your teen about things he's doing right, versus what he's doing wrong?*

> "Don't make a big deal out of little things! There are so many things that are big deals that it's wise to let slide the things that honestly won't matter a few weeks from now or a few years from now. Save the battles for the things that really matter and learn to tolerate the rest."
>
> —A PARENT

Many teens say they only hear their parents tell them what they're doing wrong. Do you cheer your teen when he does the right thing, even if he *should* have been doing it right all along?

7. *Is every word from you an instruction?*

"Make your bed. Wash your hair. Pick up your room. Don't talk like that to your mother. Put on a different shirt for church." Sound familiar?

8. *When you need to ask for something, do you use terms like "Please," "Thank you," and "You're welcome"?*

Do you use the words you want them to use with you? Or is politeness only for strangers?

9. *Do you treat your teen the way you want to be treated?*

If you don't want her going through your dresser drawers, do you go through hers? Exceptions might be necessary if you have reason to suspect drug use, for example, but do you otherwise assume your teen deserves the same privacy, patience, and praise you do?

10. *How often do you ask your teen how she feels about something?*

And when you do, do you respond with kindness and clarifying questions?

11. *Are you grumpy or annoyed when your teen tries to talk with you?*

If he approaches you at a bad time, do you try to take a deep breath and give him the attention he needs? If you absolutely can't talk then, do you set up a better time and follow through?

12. *Does spending time with your teen seem like an intrusion, an annoying necessity, or a privilege?*

Your attitude, spoken or not, will come across. Parents who don't see their kids as exciting people with new ideas, refreshing emotions, and great potential will see less and less of them.

13. *Do you talk about your teen in derogatory terms, even when she's within earshot?*

Ever find yourself on the phone, chuckling with a friend over a "minor" problem your teen found painful? How did you feel when you realized your teen was listening? More importantly, how did your teen feel?

14. *Do you have "cute" put-downs about teenagers decorating your home?*

Would you want to visit someone who had a sign on the wall that said, "Friends are the bane of my life—but they do cause me to fall on my knees and pray"? Does that plaque or refrigerator magnet saying "I'm insane—I have teenagers" make your kid feel loved or ridiculed?

15. *Do you share "prayer requests" about your teen without permission?*

Do you say, "Will you pray for me? John has been so annoying these past few days"? Would you say that about your spouse, especially if he or she were sitting next to you?

16. *Have you ever called your teen a name—brat, slut, stupid, dork, skinny, liar?*

If so, is your teen trying to "live up to" that label?

17. *Are you trying to control your teen instead of influencing him?*

If so, is he resentfully buckling under, or revolting to prove "you can't control me"? Are those really the results you want?

18. *Is your treatment of your teen based on conditional love?*

Does your teen really believe nothing can end your relationship, or does she feel she's always on probation?

19. *Do you try to hide or excuse your weaknesses as a parent?*

If so, why? Don't you have strengths, too—strengths that can help you work on your weaknesses? Do you believe God can step in and do something amazing despite your shortcomings (2 Corinthians 12:9, Romans 8:26) if you ask Him?

20. *Are you demanding respect instead of earning it?*

Do you live what you believe? Or do you speak about integrity but lie to the telemarketer on the phone? Respect from teens is earned by being authentic—not by saying, "Because I'm your father, that's why."

What Kinds of Pressures Are on You?

Let's take a break for a minute. Instead of spotlighting your possible flaws, let's consider factors that may be shoving you close to—or over—the edge. You may be able to do something about these stresses, too.

1. *What kind of baggage are you carrying?*

Are you dragging around pieces of your past? That load can affect how you relate to your teen. If you're a woman who got pregnant before marriage, you might fear the same thing will happen to your daughter—and hush any mention of her blossoming sexuality. If you're a guy who desperately wanted to make the high school football team but couldn't, you might push your son to achieve that goal even though he'd rather spend his time building computers.

> "I [kept trying] to be more and more of an authoritarian, which would just result in a greater level of conflict."
> —A PARENT

2. Are you schedule-stretched?

No matter how hard we try to drop anchor, most of us in this society scream across the water of life at lightning speed. Jobs, home, school, church—even good things suck up too much time and energy. The casualties are our teens, who come home to empty homes or drained parents.

3. Are you struggling to survive?

If it's all you can do to pay the rent and put macaroni on the table—or if even that is out of the question right now—the anxiety doesn't leave you with much emotional strength to give your teen. Neither does having a spouse deployed to the battlefield, or a car that can't be counted on to get you to work. Fear can shape whether you're "there" for your teen, and not in a good way.

4. Are you a single parent?

No job is harder—especially if the other parent has died or has chosen to abandon you. My wife and my mother were raised in single-parent homes, and both are among the most incredible women I've ever met. But raising a teen in that situation is a challenge that makes the Super Bowl look easy.

5. Do custody arrangements shorten time with your teen?

If you don't have your teen 24/7, you have less influence. That doesn't mean you can't accomplish plenty in your home, on your "watch." But you may have to pay extra attention to how you're using those precious hours.

6. *Do you have health limitations?*

Chronic illness, disability, a life-threatening condition—only someone who's been through it knows how completely these things can take over. During my treatment for leukemia, you can be sure I discovered boundaries on my energy and ability. God isn't limited by those limitations, but you may have to find alternatives to bungee-jumping with your teen.

7. *Are you on a tight budget?*

Cheaper alternatives—a camping weekend, a game of Monopoly—may be just as effective as a trip to Universal Studios when it comes to bonding with your son or daughter. But always having to say no to your first choice—and your teen's—can wear you down.

8. *Is your teen reluctant to let you into his life?*

One youth leader says the teen world is one into which you need to be invited. If you long for that invitation but never seem

> "[I thought,] 'Well, [sending my child away] is certainly not something that I'm going to have to do. You know, I can fix that. I'm a fixer.' So it really came to just being humble enough to say, 'You know, I think I've tried everything and talked to everybody I know, and I don't seem to have the ability to work this out'—which is kind of ironic since I seemingly work out more complex issues for people, even in relationships, on a daily basis."
>
> —A PARENT

to get one, you may feel pressured to crash the party. You probably know that forcing your way through the Great Wall isn't the
answer, but the sense of urgency makes you want to try.

9. *Are you worn out by your teen's normal growing-up process?*

As your teen matures, certain shifts are predictable, desired,
and irreversible. Dependence turns to independence; following
rules gives way to considering advice. If you fight this process,
you're bound to lose—and gain a lot of wrinkles and gray hair. As
counselor Tim Sanford says, "These things happen *faster* than the
parent wants them to, and *slower* than the teen wants them to."

10. *Are you trying to do the impossible?*

As Tim Sanford also reminds us, it's not our job to make sure
our teens turn out right. We should feed, clothe, model, teach,
correct, discipline, set limits, encourage, pray. But we're not
responsible for their choices. Not even God stopped His first children from picking the wrong fruit in the Garden of Eden. Trying
to outdo Him is a sure recipe for exhaustion and defeat.

If you wrestle with one or more of these ten challenges, you
may tend to be short-tempered or disinterested in having a relationship with your teen. It's vital to gain a little relief, which may
mean sitting with a trusted friend, pastor, or counselor to create
a blueprint that helps you accept and do the most with what you
have.

What Kind of Plans Do You Have?

Let's look at one more aspect of parenting in which you have a
majority vote.

What's your goal for your teen?

Is it to be in charge of his life? Maybe you'd like to be able to say, "My child listens to my directions and automatically responds, or does so with a little prodding."

Is it to be the main voice in your teen's ear? Perhaps you want a kid who'll do what you ask in his choice of friends, spending leisure time and money, and picking a college and career.

Is it to have a constantly deepening, thoroughly harmonious relationship? Maybe you envision long talks over lemonade, followed by, "Wow, Mom, you've really given me something to think about."

How realistic are those goals?

Not very. Neither are the other goals many parents set for themselves: fixing a teen, making up for lost time, undoing mistakes, or making it all better. Shooting for targets like those will only lead to frustration and failure—and sometimes even incite more rebellion.

Counselor Tim Sanford suggests some reasonable goals:

1. *Have as few rules as possible.* Make them specific, measurable, and enforceable. Their purpose should be to keep chaos out and safety in. Think: If you could have only five rules in your family, what would they be?

2. *Do what you can, not what you can't.* You can't heal all wounds—and you shouldn't. Rescuing your teen from the consequences of all her actions will only make life more difficult for her in the future.

3. *Begin to show with your words and your life that you care.* Talk is one thing, actions another. Align the two and you'll make a powerful difference in your teen's life.

4. *Start letting your teen know who you really are.* Believe it or not, he's interested. He's watched you from a distance and with a child's-eye view. Now he has the chance to really get to know you, what you believe, and why.

5. *Communicate with your teen as much as she'll let you.* Don't force conversations. Let them happen in the car, over dinner, while doing chores together.

6. *Make the relationship about your teen, not you.* I'm as guilty as anyone when it comes to thinking it's all about me and my comfort. It's really about my young person's struggles and joy, and letting her know I love, accept, and appreciate her.

In other words, do the best you can with *your* side of the relationship.

You're on Your Way

So, did that hurt?

Not too much, I hope. But maybe you've seen a few places where you've contributed to unhappiness at home. Maybe you've found some things to work on.

You can't fix your teen, but you can take some mighty strides toward a better relationship than you ever thought possible. You've just taken the first step—an honest look in the mirror.

"Set the rules. Enforce the rules. But be sure the rules aren't stupid. Have a reason for everything you do. Go back to what you really want for yourself, your kids, and your relationship. Pray with your kid. Talk with your kid, not at your kid."

—A PARENT

What's the next step?

It's one of the most basic things you can imagine—and one that so many moms and dads are too busy to think about. Turn to the next chapter, put up your feet, and take time . . . to take time.

4

Come Home, It's Suppertime

One thing that is so important to me is time! I don't get to spend a whole lot of time with my dad because he is always working. I just wish that he could be home more so I could talk to him more and actually spend time with him. It's just like with God, if you don't spend time talking to Him and getting to know Him, then you aren't going to have a close relationship with Him. My mother and I, on the other hand, have a very close relationship. We will go get Cokes after school, go to the mall, go to Wal-Mart. . . . I believe that spending time is one of the biggest things in a child's life.

—A TEEN

What does it take to wake us parents up?

In my case, the alarm went off three times.

It happened one summer before my kids were teenagers, and it showed me that my priorities were way out of whack.

Alarm #1: Nine-year-old Jamie came to my office one day. "Dad," she said, brown eyes luminous, "when can I get an appointment?"

Alarm #2: A few weeks later, younger daughter Courtney was in a camp next door to the one I was directing. Even though she'd been raised around Kamp, she got really homesick. When the week was almost over, Courtney's counselor knelt down to encourage her: "In two days you'll get to go home and see your dad."

Courtney replied, "I *never* get to see my dad."

Soon the director of Courtney's Kamp marched into my office. He sat down and declared, "Until you change your priorities, I'm not moving."

"*I wish [my parents] would, every once in a while, spend an afternoon with me alone.*"

—A TEEN

Alarm #3: Shortly after that, five-year-old Brady's babysitter taught him how to ride a bike—because I wasn't there. When I got home for lunch, Brady said proudly, "Hey, Dad, I learned to ride my bike this morning."

"Wow, Brady!" I answered. "That's great. I'd like to see you ride this afternoon."

"That's okay, Dad. You can come see me next fall."

"I'd like to see you this afternoon."

"No, Dad. You *work* in the summer."

That three-alarm blaze left me feeling a pain I can't express. I now knew the loss my kids were feeling.

Dad was too busy. That summer I made some staunch commitments to reprioritize, and spent extraordinary amounts of time with my kids from then on. Still, my time spent away from my family brought scars that will take a lifetime to repair.

For most parents, the wake-up call probably doesn't come as bluntly as mine did. But countless conversations I've had with teens have made it clear that when we don't spend enough time with our sons and daughters, we pay the price in fractured relationships.

Who are the happiest kids I see? The ones whose parents are

"there" for them. These teens see their parents at every turn. They know they can reach their parents when they need to ask that burning question. They don't have to worry about "quality" time versus "quantity" time; they've got both.

The unhappy kids say their parents are distant, working too hard, bent over the computer keyboard, gone to committee meetings. They desperately want their parents at their games, plays, and concerts.

Find that hard to believe? After all, isn't it natural for teens to start pulling away from their parents?

Sure. But most aren't ready to be completely free just yet. They're like birds learning to fly—taking off for a few loops, then coming back to the nest where they hope to find a firm foundation before taking off again.

Listen to Kara, a beautiful girl who's gotten involved with alcohol and has become too intimate with boys:

"I tried to explain to Mom the reason why I felt I wanted to

> *"My dad . . . chooses us over his work, so that we can spend more time with him and grow up with a dad in our house. He could be making a lot more money, but instead he has been our coach for volleyball, baseball, and basketball all through junior high and high school. He is my hero! . . . My mom is the best mom, too, because she juggles being a mom of four kids and owning her own store. And yet she makes it to all of our games and activities. Plus doing laundry and keeping our house clean."*
> —A TEEN

do these things was because I felt no love at home. I mean, my mom promised to come to my [horseback] riding lessons, and watch me ride or at least come to see my rodeos. Instead she would always go to my sister's tumbling classes and jump rope practices. She judges for jump rope and everything now. I didn't feel like she loved me because [she never came to my events].

"My real dad, he lives in California—and it's been a constant battle ever since they got a divorce that I always have to come see him, he won't ever come to see me. He came to see my sister three or four times. It's been very difficult because he's like if you want to see me, you have to come see me, I'm not going to come see you."

When you talk with Kara, you see the pain in her blue eyes. She's pleading for her mom and dad to come home!

Kara is desperate for love. If she doesn't get it at home, she'll numb the pain through alcohol and get lost in the arms of any boy who'll take her in. And believe me, plenty of boys are eager to give "love" to lost girls.

> *"No matter how crazy or busy our lives got, we always had a sit-down dinner and made sure we spent quality time together every day. My brother and I started playing soccer when we were both five and played a lot of travel soccer. [Our parents] always made it to every game. . . . They always made sure I got to my piano lessons and were there for recitals. . . . My parents also endured the five-hour summer swim meets, and even helped out as timers. They gave so much time and made so many sacrifices for my brother and me."*
>
> —A TEEN

Is Anybody There?

Do you spend too much time away from home? When you're there, are you available physically and emotionally? Or are you wrapped up in television, moonlighting, or restoring an old Corvette?

If you're there when the kids get home from school, do they have a listening, caring parent to talk with? Or do they have to stand in the kitchen, shifting from foot to foot, hoping you'll get off the phone?

If you get home later, do you push aside attempts at closeness, your face and body language like an electrified fence? Do you mumble a hello to your kids and demand they give a respectful, clear response? If your teen has a concert at school, do you beg off because you're too tired?

If so, it's not surprising. Parenting a teen—not to mention keeping up with the bills—is exhausting work. Just when you thought your kids would need less from you, you find they need more.

And time is what they need most. Quality *and* quantity time. I watch the effects of time spent with kids every year at Kanakuk Kamps, where teens spend 24 hours a day with counselors who affirm them individually at least 10 times daily. You can almost see those young people growing more open and confident right before your eyes.

Wouldn't you like to see that happen with your son or daughter, too?

Parents Who Came Home

Coming home can be hard. It requires sacrifice.

Jim Harrold is another dad who did what it took to spend

more time with his kids. A longtime missionary, he found his work in Latin America sending him up the ladder of success. His leadership and speaking skills were in demand worldwide. His work was God's work—but he had to come home.

Jim writes: "I remember that [my daughter] Erin's birthday was a difficult date to keep free. I always had the best and most invitations to be gone on that day. But when she was ten or so, she told me I had already missed two or three birthdays. When I realized she kept track, I made up my mind to never be gone on her birthday as long as she was living at home. That was not an easy commitment to keep. I think it was important, whether or not Erin noticed. It was important to me to help me keep my focus in the right place and to value my daughters above my work."

Other parents have made more sweeping changes for their kids' sake. One mom tells her story:

My husband and I went to a Bible study group that met in someone's home. The house was big and gorgeous, and I was jealous the moment I walked in the door. *Oh, if I had a kitchen like this . . . Oh, if only we had a big coat closet like this . . . Oh, if only my kids had a big basement filled with cool stuff . . .* etc., etc. The hostess's husband is a lawyer and my husband is a lawyer, and I kept thinking, *This just isn't fair.* The third couple [in the group] also produced a large income from the husband's work.

As we got into the Bible study, we were all sharing tough things we've had to deal with in our lives, and both of the other wives talked a long time about what it has been like to essentially raise their children by themselves. They went on and on about how early their husbands leave in the morning, and they don't get home until well after the kids are in bed at night, and they work all weekend, etc. Suddenly I was filled with shame for every jealous thought I had had before.

My husband worked at a law firm for one year after he graduated, and then we both said the life we wanted was not one in which you have to make a choice between your career and your family (this is required in the part of the country in which we live).

We chose family, so we made some substantial changes. He moved to a family-oriented Christian non-profit agency to serve as their CFO/legal counsel. He loves what he does (and he's outstanding at it), but he also took a tremendous dip in pay. We live in a little house that needs a lot of work, and we both drive older cars. We don't have a lot of fancy toys. He does not get bonuses or giant raises or wonderful benefits.

But this is our life. Today, after the kids were on the bus, we cuddled and talked for a long time before he started getting ready for work. (I think he finally headed to the office at 10:15 A.M.!) On Wednesday, he is taking the day off to help me with my job. This weekend, he took the kids to his mom's to give me some quiet so I could finish my freelance work. For a week and a half, he went in late every morning and came home early every evening so that I could do what I needed to do on my project.

He takes the day off whenever the kids have a field trip so that he can go along. He has done community theater with them, is home to have dinner and help with homework most nights, and only occasionally has to go in for a few hours on the weekend. If they are off from school on a workday, he'll as often as not bring them to work with him and let them hang out while he does his job. He is such a huge part of their lives and mine.

After that Bible study, I thought about what I really wanted: fancy kitchen or Dad on field trip? Big coat closet or husband at dinner table? Toys in big basement or help with my career?

I think I must find a way to remind myself how fortunate I am. My heart aches for the lawyer's wife in her big house. I'm just so glad to get a reminder of the choice we made and how it has played out. Family or career? Give me family. Even if it means we're drinking out of jelly jars, at least we're all drinking together.

I have a friend who's a major-league surgeon. He came to me after realizing he was losing touch with his teens. He could see them frozen in the distance, almost like Tevye in *Fiddler on the Roof.*

I suggested he come home.

He looked at me, his face etched with despair. "But I can't."

I knew what he meant. His skills were in constant demand at all hours of the day and night.

So I challenged him with what I hoped would be a reasonable goal. "Try to give 10 percent of each day to your kids. Just 10 percent."

He did. To his astonishment, his teens began to respond. What he thought he'd lost forever, he regained—when he gave only 10 percent of his time.

I'd tried this principle at home, too. After pouring myself into my job every day and coming home with a chip on my shoulder and looking for a soft place to lie down, I'd had nothing left to give my kids. One day I'd slithered home, anxious to do nothing, when a thought floated into my head: *Save 10 percent.*

That sounded reasonable, doable. So I set myself a goal of reserving 10 percent of my energy for my children. My new top calling was to be a dad.

I used that 10 percent with my teens—shooting hoops, running pass patterns, and listening to a squawking saxophone. In their hearts they knew I thought they were special, that I valued them.

A Time to Mend

I'm not the only one who thinks it's worth it to sacrifice your time during the few years your teen has left at home. Listen to this girl's story:

"My mom drove us to and from school every day. That meant at least an hour a day in the car. It was so great because, being the

> "[My parents] were willing to drop anything at any time to be with us and to help us. They loved being at home and spending time with us whether it was playing a game, my dad reading us a book, watching a movie, or playing in the yard. The main reason I can explain how my parents were there for me is that when I remember my life growing up, and even recently, they fill up so many of those memories. They lived and breathed our family."
>
> —A TEEN

incredibly wise woman that she is, my mom would listen to what
was going on. Then she would offer her best advice for a problem.
This way, we all learned to
trust my mom, and we
weren't ever afraid to tell her
about something that had
happened. My mom has
always encouraged us to talk
to her because she knows
that we're not perfect and
we're going to screw up

"I learned quality time only happens
with quantity time. There is a window
of opportunity when a kid will talk . . .
and if you aren't there when they feel
like talking . . . it ain't gonna happen.
I tried to be there whenever I could."

—A PARENT

sometimes. She's extremely good at waiting until we're ready to
tell her what's on our minds, and she just listens and then gives us
advice or takes action if it's needed."

It takes time to be that kind of mentor to your teen. Here's
how one parent put it: "Whenever there was a choice between
being with the kids and doing something else, the best choice was
being with them."

Want to see a change in your teen's behavior? Make the first
move by coming home.

5

Having to Say You're Sorry

"I'm sorry. What I did was wrong." Those words are rarely
heard by anyone. They are heard even less by children. Then
there is the ultimate rarity when a child hears it from their
parents. When my mom or dad tells me that, it changes
things a bit. For a moment, I have to put aside my anger
and my hurt and change my view toward them. For a
moment, they are at the same level as me. I do not see
them as a figure of authority, but as a friend asking for
forgiveness. The reason that I no longer see them as a
figure of authority is because they are vulnerable. They no
longer have the "parent wall" surrounding them. It makes
me feel better when my parents apologize because they
are realizing their mistakes and are righting a wrong.
I see them as more than just a parent, but a friend as well.
Apologies from my parents are rare, but when I get them,
I never have any trouble saying, "You're forgiven."

—A TEEN

What are the words that can change a teen's life?

"I'm sorry."

"I apologize for _____."

"I was wrong. Will you forgive me?"

Need proof? Take a look at this teen's story:

Okay, so about a year ago, my dad and I went to
Nebraska—and it was a big deal because I had never been
alone with my dad. So I was really nervous to do it. And
we went and I don't know what happened, but I just totally
lost it and everything came out. And we were in the car,
which really wasn't smart because if things would've gotten
bad I couldn't really escape or anything, you know.

So we talked about it and actually he apologized for
everything. He started crying, and I've never seen my dad
cry. He started crying and said that he was sorry that he'd
missed the past 18 years of my life. There was no way he
could get them back. That was really hard to do, but it was
such a relief to finally know that at least he realized that he
wasn't there and he realized he wasn't a dad to me at all.
So, that was good to hear, especially the apology part.

The most powerful words we can say to our kids are also the
most humbling—and sometimes the most painful.

Sorry Seems to Be the Hardest Word

Nobody likes to apologize. It's embarrassing. We feel ashamed,
sad, foolish. It's tough to get those words out, even if they're the
only way to move beyond the wreckage of a parent-teen conflict
and start healing.

Why is that difficulty multiplied when we need to apologize to our own kids? See whether any of these reasons might apply to you.

1. Until now, your child has looked up to you. Asking forgiveness is an admission that you're not perfect—which implies that maybe you don't always make the best choices as a parent. You're afraid this will cause your teen to doubt all your decisions, or to find further excuse to defy you.

2. It can be humiliating to admit you're wrong. It feels like assigning yourself to the penalty box. The truth is that it takes strength to acknowledge your faults, and can help your teen relate to you as a fellow mistake-maker—but it's not much fun.

3. You want to model perfection so your teen will strive for a higher goal. Unfortunately, models of perfection discourage kids who feel like they're messing up constantly. If they can't be perfect, why try at all?

4. You fear that if you admit you're flawed, your teen won't respect you anymore. Actually, the opposite is true. Kids say they respect their parents *more* when they apologize.

> "My parenting methodology was the drill sergeant—you know, 'This is what you're going to do and this is how you're going to do it. And if you don't do it I'm going to be really mad at you. And there's going to be some sort of punishment.' You know, that whole mentality doesn't really show any kind of love—and they don't really get that you love them. They begin to resent you."
>
> —A PARENT

Why Apologize?

Does asking forgiveness really reduce the distance between parents and teens? Can it defuse rebellion? These teens seem to think so:

The fact that my mom is willing to humble herself and admit that she has made a mistake helps me to respect her a lot. It makes it so much easier for me to apologize and want to change when she will meet me in the middle. It also makes it easier to identify with the things she tells me and helps me to pay attention to her advice by her taking away an attitude of superiority.

It greatly encouraged me that my dad thought it was necessary to confess his sin. It set before me an example of what is true and right. I will never forget this.

When my parents apologize to me it just lets me know that we all make mistakes when we're young and old—and helps me realize that we're all in the same boat. It helps me see that they are trying hard, too.

When my parents tell me they're sorry, I feel as if they really do care about me and how their mistake affected me. It reminds me that they are not perfect either and that they are still learning from mistakes. Above all, their apology reminds me that they really do love and care for me.

My parents were always very quick to apologize. This is probably the reason that I don't remember any exact incidents where they hurt me.

My parents have never had a problem with saying, "Sorry." It never made me feel better right away, but I couldn't stay mad at them. And it made it a lot easier to say that I was sorry when I screwed up.

When my mom apologized, it helped me to see that she understood me. It made me feel closer to her.

When my dad apologized to me, this greatly improved our relationship. I stopped thinking of him as perfect and started thinking of him as a human. When that happened, I realized that I could hang out with him and be friends.

> "I get a chance to come up and live with my dad, [and] he doesn't even want to hang out with me. And he doesn't even say, 'Let's you and me go to the show together. Let's me and you just go hit the town.' It's always, 'Brad, here's some money. You go out and you go do what you want. I'm going to go do what I want. I'll see you when I see you.' Last conversation I had with my dad: 'Here's some money. If you need to get bailed out of jail, give me a call. Other than that, see you when I see you.'"
>
> —A TEEN

I don't know about you. But I can't read those words without wanting to figure out something to apologize to my kids for!

Where Do I Begin?

When it comes to asking forgiveness, the hardest thing to do is take the first step.

1. *Look into your teen's eyes.* Don't glance around the floor or wipe the counter or dust the furniture while you're talking. Don't sit at your computer. Find a quiet spot away from other family members and make eye contact. Your teen may be afraid at first that you're going to lecture her about something she did, so don't be surprised if she squirms a bit.

> "I would cry growing up, and my father would say, 'Be a man! Men don't cry!' And that's such a lie."
>
> —A TEEN

2. *Define the wrong; don't leave it vague.* Name what you did that you shouldn't have done. For example, "I'm sorry I called you a 'stupid kid.' That was insulting—and untrue, too." Or, "I'm sorry I didn't believe you when you told me your teacher was being unfair. I didn't take the time to hear you out."

3. *Say those difficult words.* "I'm sorry. Will you forgive me?"

4. *Be quiet.* Your teen might respond by granting forgiveness. He might be stunned and say nothing. If he's still angry, he might say, "No."

What should you do if you get a negative reponse?

Smile. Pat him on the shoulder or knee and say, "I love you."

Then walk away—not angrily, but knowing that what you did to hurt your teen might take time to heal. Allow him that time.

After all, if someone dropped a concrete block and broke your toe, would an apology take away the pain?

The Truth Will Set You Free

Asking forgiveness opens up plenty of possibilities—all of them good. Here's what happened when one father took that awkward step. His son tells the story:

> My dad asked to sit and talk with me. And I was like, "Yeah, sure." I sat down thinking this was just going to be another lip-service thing. My dad said, "Listen, I know you hate me. You've got a lot of reasons to hate me. I want to apologize for not being the type of father that you needed. I just wanted to get everything out on the floor and I just want you to tell me everything."

"I wish we'd been less judgmental of their friends and just others in general who believed differently than we do. I think we tried to protect them from anything that didn't line up with our Christian worldview, and it ended up making us seem (well, maybe we were) narrow-minded and uncompassionate. Thankfully, our adult kids have a lot more compassion and mercy on others than we did. I'm thankful that, in spite of us, they seem to see other people the way Jesus does."

—A PARENT

My dad was just so sincere about the whole thing. And he hugged me and grabbed me and said, "You're my boy . . . you'll always be my boy."

What was so different was just—one, he was hugging me different. It wasn't the hugs before, just a courteous hug. He grabbed me and embraced me like a brother. He embraced me like Jesus would have embraced one of His disciples.

> "I never really felt 'I love you.'"
>
> —A TEEN

Or like the Prodigal Son's father embraced *his* boy (Luke 15). As you may recall, that led to a whole bunch of partying.

Forgiveness is like that.

6

Seventy Times Seven

No one in my family has a very good relationship with my dad (if you can even call it a relationship), and I think one of the big reasons for this is because he likes to make it seem that he was always perfect and he gave no room for us to mess up.

—A TEEN

If he did something that was hurtful to me, I let him know that was hurtful—but I still loved him, and that I wouldn't hold it against him. I just never brought it up again.

—A PARENT

Forgiveness runs both ways. Sometimes we moms and dads need to be on the receiving end—and sometimes we need to dispense it to our teens.

That's a tall order, especially if our kids are in the middle of rebelling. On a scale of 1 to 10, with 10 meaning "impossible," how easy would it be for you to forgive your teen in each of the following situations?

1. Driving at night on an icy road, he smashes your car into a telephone pole.

2. Driving while talking on a cell phone, he smashes your car into a telephone pole.

3. Driving drunk, he smashes your car into a telephone pole.

4. Driving without a license, he smashes your car into a telephone pole.

Let's assume he survives the accident without a scratch. Now, how easy would it be to forgive if your teen didn't even apologize? What if you suspected he'd go out and do the same thing again if given half a chance?

> "He did some crazy stuff, but he always convinced us that it was the last time. And the younger one was even better at it."
>
> —A PARENT

Maybe the thought of forgiving in those circumstances is enough to send your blood pressure through the roof. Yet Jesus commands us to forgive an offense at least 490 times (Matthew 18:21-22)! It hardly seems fair, does it?

There's got to be a reason why God is so strict on this point. To find it, let's start by figuring out what forgiveness is . . . and isn't.

Forgiveness Is for Giving

Forgiving is a *requirement* which, if you neglect it, will come back to bite you when you least want it to—in eternity. Jesus tells us in Matthew 6:14-15 that if we don't forgive, God won't forgive us. That's not a happy thought. If you're like me, you've got so many sins trailing behind you, you'd be embarrassed if anyone found out about them.

But forgiving isn't as easy as saying the words "I forgive you."

And saying the words doesn't sweep away the feelings or the fallout.

Here are seven things to remember about forgiveness.

1. *Forgiveness may not happen overnight.* We can mumble the words, shout them enthusiastically, speak them through tears, even sing them. But what if, the next morning, the pain is still there? What if the "magic" hasn't worked?

Forgiving someone is a process. Sometimes it takes months or years for the feelings to follow. And don't expect to forget what happened right away.

2. *Forgiveness is worth praying about.* One of the worst things that ever hit me was a time when I felt betrayed. It hurt me to the core. I didn't want to forgive, not at the gut level. Hard as I tried, nothing got rid of the pain. I wanted the person to suffer. If I forgave, everybody would be happy except me.

I had to pray that God would give me the desire to forgive. In time, He did. As a result, I found a freedom that has helped me forgive ever since.

3. *Forgiveness is not excusing a wrong.* I used to think that saying "I forgive you" was the same as saying "It's no big deal." But that's not true.

"I forgive you" doesn't mean, "It's okay that you cheated on a test." It doesn't mean, "It's okay that you yelled at me and called me an idiot." It doesn't mean, "It's okay to trash my reputation."

The offense *does* matter. Wrong is wrong; sin is sin. It matters so much that Scripture says, "The wages of sin is death" (Romans 6:23). It matters so much that Jesus had to die to pay for that sin.

A man was arrested for repeatedly molesting his niece. After he was convicted, the time came for the judge to sentence him.

The man's wife protested the jail term, saying, "Where's the forgiveness?"

The molester's daughter-in-law stood up. "Forgiveness does not eliminate the need for this man to be put away to protect the other grandchildren," she said. "Forgiveness does not negate consequences or justice."

She had that right. Our earthly laws call for consequences. So does God's law.

4. *Forgiveness isn't pretending something didn't happen.* It's not brushing things under the rug. It's facing the wrong head on, acknowledging that there is something to forgive.

5. *Forgiveness doesn't come without a price.* Who pays it? Jesus. He's already done that on the Cross for *all* sin for *all* time. Whether we accept His offer of rescue is up to us.

> "[Our daughter was saying,] 'I'm going to be basically a jerk, and I'm not responsible for my actions. I'm immature, I'm going to act immature, and basically I'm going to ruin my parents' life.'"
>
> —A PARENT

It's tempting, even as we "forgive" our teens, to try to "make them pay." But they can't, and neither can we. We can impose penalties that help our teens not to repeat their mistakes, but the only One who can settle accounts with God has already done that.

6. *Forgiveness means letting God control what happens.* If you don't forgive, it'll cost you. The price will be bitterness and resentment if you hold a grudge or hang on to the idea of getting revenge. Let God control the outcome, though, and you'll be free.

This means not keeping track of whether God is dealing with your teen as you would. Man, that's hard! I don't know about you, but there are moments when I don't trust God that much! Still, "payback" only makes things worse.

7. *Sometimes we need to forgive without being asked.* You may suffer because of the attitude, choices, and even cruelty of a son or daughter who'll never apologize. It's up to you to forgive without being asked. Remember: Do what you can with *your* side of the relationship.

Sometimes this process must take place daily, on your knees, tears dropping to the floor—knowing the person who hurt you may never admit it. When that person is your teen, you may have to give up the hope that you'll be vindicated by an apology.

Forgiveness and Tough Love

But how can a parent keep forgiving a teen without seeming to condone his behavior? What about "tough love"?

As counselor Tim Sanford reminds us, forgiveness isn't for the benefit of the person who did the wrong. It has nothing to do with letting the offender off the hook. It's for the benefit of the person who's been wronged. It provides a way for that person to heal—by acknowledging the offense and letting go of it by giving it over to God.

Tim points out that confrontation, in the form of "tough love," is designed for the benefit of the offender. It's an attempt to show him that what he did was wrong, encouraging him to correct his behavior and live a healthier life that pleases God.

Forgiveness and tough love aren't opposites. They aren't mutually exclusive. As a parent, you'll often be doing both at the same time.

Tim uses the example of a teenager named Andy (not his real

name). Let's say Andy develops the regular, and very bad, habit of lying. His parents are hurt every time they're lied to. Still, for their own sake, they forgive Andy repeatedly—at least 70 times 7.

What they *don't* do is naively *trust* Andy time and again. They confront every lie they encounter and mete out a consequence— even if the consequence doesn't seem to "work" in the sense of changing Andy's actions.

They remind Andy that trust is always *earned.* Trust will come after Andy proves himself trustworthy—worthy of trust. They explain to him the following progression:

> "He'd tell any story he thought would work. He'd just change the story like a chameleon."
>
> —A PARENT

1. A natural consequence of lying is broken trust.

2. The consequence of broken trust is not being trusted.

3. The consequence of not being trusted is that Andy won't be allowed to use the car for the next month. That's because they can't trust him to tell the truth about where he'll be or what he'll be doing.

Andy's parents forgive—*and* they exercise tough love by bringing consequences to bear on him.

Tim explains that many parents mistakenly feel they *must* trust their teenager—or that by trusting their teen despite his behavior, they will somehow make him trustworthy. They trust an untrustworthy person, only to be hurt again and again.

Does that mean you should expect perfection before trusting your teen? No. As Tim says, teenagers are still fairly immature. We're talking about a general pattern of being responsible.

Forgiving a teen like Andy, coupled with "tough love" confrontation, shows him what the grownup world is really like. It also saves his parents a whole lot of extra heartache.

As You Have Received

How many times have you needed forgiveness from others? How about that harsh word said in haste and anger, that speeding on the freeway, that blank CD you took home from the office?

No one deserves to be forgiven. Yet Christ died for all (2 Corinthians 5:15; 1 Peter 3:18), including you and your teen.

Your teen needs to know she's forgiven. Guilt can eat her alive, and your condemnation will only make her feel weaker. Next time temptation comes, she'll be even more likely to trip again.

Set your child free from this vicious cycle! Offer forgiveness. Don't bring up past failures in "subtle" ways like these:

"I've told you that 50 times."

"When will you ever learn?"

"Can't you see what I've been trying to teach you this whole year?"

> "He had gotten into some serious drugs. He was addicted to coke . . . snorted heroin at least a couple of times . . . he'd done mushrooms. He was taking drugs while maintaining a darn good GPA at a private school. He was voted on the Honor Council."
>
> —A PARENT

"Why do you keep doing that?"

"You really have been a disappointment to me lately."

"Don't you ever listen?"

If discipline is required, use it firmly, carefully, lovingly, prayerfully—and then *move on*. Remember Romans 8:1-2: "Therefore, there is now no condemnation for those who are in Christ Jesus, because through Christ Jesus the law of the Spirit of life set me free from the law of sin and death."

> *"Remember your kid is not evil . . . just changing . . . and most likely has no idea what he or she is inadvertently doing to the relationship. Don't hold grudges. That doesn't mean that bad behavior goes ignored or unpunished . . . just that you need to have a true, two-way dialog about how life is going, what you both want, and how you'll get there. Be ready to have this conversation frequently."*
>
> —A PARENT

7

Calm Down and Clam Up

*My dad has always been very condemning in his words and
the way he relates to us. Whenever we tell him about what's
actually going on in our lives, he comes up with ways to tear
us down or condemn our actions. He views our behavior as
less than perfect and it becomes so annoying that none of
us talk to him anymore. I hate having him comment on
things that I do, so I would rather not talk at all.*

—A TEEN

How do you rebuild a relationship with a teen who's distant or
rebellious?

It can't happen without communication.

I'm not talking about the kind of speech that passes for conversation in many homes:

"Get off the Internet! I'm expecting a phone call!"

"You can turn your house into a garbage dump when you
grow up, but for now you'd better pick those cracker crumbs out
of the carpet."

"It won't kill you to ask the teacher how to do that algebra."

"When was the last time you had a shower?"

I'm talking about the kind of communication that leads to closeness, intimacy, connecting at a deeper level. It's the kind of relating that's hard to do when kids are little—and that many parents don't even try to do when their kids are teens.

Those parents are missing out. You don't have to be among them.

Letting Your Teen into Your Heart

Believe it or not, most teens want a closer relationship with their parents. It's easy to forget that when there's so much growling going on, but the fact is that adolescents are becoming people you can really get to know—and who can get to know you. Parents who don't realize this may, without meaning to, push their teens away. The teens, in turn, push back.

I have great relationships with all my adult children. But it wasn't always that way. I had to learn to let my kids into my heart.

That wasn't too hard when it came to sharing daily joys and sadness. I could tell them what it was like to be 50, or that I'd had a bad day. I could come home jumping up and down, waving new projects. But when it came to revealing that I'm a fallen man, it was much tougher.

"They could actually listen to me, instead of them always saying their opinion."

—A TEEN

I knew that humility was the key that would open their hearts. So prayerfully, carefully, and age appropriately, I talked about my first marriage—which ended in divorce. I talked about some of my other failings, too.

It was hard to share my failures in a constructive way. I wanted to be a role model, to give them someone to look up to. But heroes aren't real unless they have cracks and scars.

Those discussions were pretty raw. But they were good, and strengthened the bond between my kids and me.

This can be a scary thing for parents. When it comes to communication, many of us would rather loiter around the surface where it's "safe." But there are five levels of communication, and it's our loss if we never try to experience all of them with our teens:

> *"Sometimes it's better for . . . parents to start talking than expecting [their] kids to come. Because [kids] don't have the guts to come up and say, 'Hey, I need to talk.'"*
>
> —A TEEN

1. *Small talk.* This is the level we use on airplanes, or in the grocery store line.

2. *Sharing ideas.* We do this in the workplace, or at the church committee meeting. We test the waters, but the concepts are still distanced from who we really are.

3. *Voicing opinions.* We open the door a little and let others step into the entryway. We let them know what we think on controversial issues.

4. *Exposing emotions.* This is the level teen girls might call "best friends." You can be silly, sad, angry—and still connect with the other person. You can ask for advice, and for help with physical needs.

5. *Deepest intimacy.* This is the scariest, because you risk it all. You share the good and bad about yourself. You wonder: Will the other person still love you if she knows about your mistakes, thoughts, choices, and faults?

Most people are able to communicate on level one. They

might proceed to level two when they're comfortable. If they move to level three and their opinions are shot down, they retreat to level one.

Can We Talk?

Sadly, most parents and teens don't get past level 3. They snipe at each other's opinions instead of listening and asking respectful questions. I think you and your teen can do better.

"How?" you might ask. "How can I get to a deeper level when all I get is a grunt every day when my kid gets home from school?"

The good news is that those grunts don't necessarily mean your teen isn't interested in going deeper. When we asked a group of kids ages 13 through 17 about their concerns, they said they wanted to be able to communicate with their parents in healthy, positive ways. We got similar results in a survey at Kanakuk Kamps.

Can you believe it? Your teen wants a connection with you as much as you want one with him! I hear this at Kamp every year. Our kids *want* to talk to us!

So where's the breakdown?

Some kids just need an invitation. Others need more time to open up. Still others, though, are like the girl who said, "Every time I attempt to talk to my parents, they either yell at me before I tell my whole story or lecture me. If they'd be more open to talk with me and let me do some more talking, I'd talk with them a lot more."

Wherever you and your teen are on that spectrum of speaking, things can get better. And they will, when you take advantage of some tools parents and youth workers and counselors have been using with the kids they care about. In the rest of this chapter, let's help you and your teen get to a deeper level by stocking your communication toolbox.

Listening Tools

Here are seven ways to make sure you really hear your teen—and to make sure he or she knows it.

1. *Give him your full attention.* I know you're so busy that you hardly have a moment to yourself. But now isn't the time for multitasking. Turn off the TV, the lawnmower, the blender—whatever's competing for your ears.

2. *Reflect her emotions; don't mock them.* Teens love to see their feelings reflected in your face. It tells them you understand how they felt when the coach yelled at them today. If their emotions seem over-the-top or the reasons for them seem trivial, remember that their world is smaller than yours—which makes each event look bigger.

3. *Restate in your own words what you heard him say.* Let's say your son is dating a girl named Jen. One day he comes home and tells you about Jen flirting with his best friend. You might say, "So, what I'm hearing you say is that it really hurt when Jen looked at Brian with the look she usually gives you."
Restating helps ensure that you're truly hearing your teen. If you restate the situation incorrectly, it gives your teen a chance to re-explain, too.

> *"I hate it when I tell my parents something serious and they laugh at it."*
> —A TEEN

4. *Display attentive body language.* Skip the eye rolling, sighs, arms crossed tightly against the chest, and looking over your shoulder or into the distance. Sit cross-legged on the floor or sofa,

or turn a chair around and sit with your arms resting on the back. Lean forward slightly, nodding as appropriate.

5. *Decide to be interested in what she's saying.* This can be hard after a long day at work, coming home to a teen who wants to chatter about things that seem insignificant to you. Ask God to help you want to listen. The more you pay attention and ask clarifying questions, the more you'll find yourself interested in her life. It may help to remind yourself that what you're really interested in is *her.*

> "I like to know that what I say means something to them and that they're actually listening and trying to understand me."
>
> —A TEEN

6. *Listen to actions.* How do you do that? You notice whether your teen is slamming doors or leaving incriminating notes from a boyfriend or girlfriend around the house. Is something wrong at school? In a relationship?

7. *Be alert for moments of honesty and vulnerability.* Teens will, on occasion, break down and spill what's on their hearts. When they do, give them all the time they need to share. Then ask, "Do you want me to give suggestions or help? Or do you just want me to listen?" Instead of forcing them to retreat to level one, open the doors and let them move to level four.

Location Tools

Where you communicate with your teen is important. It can make the difference between conversation and consternation. Here are four things to keep in mind about the places in which you talk:

1. *Pick a place that provides an "out."* Kids say it's easier to talk with their parents if there's something else to focus on when things get awkward. Examples: traveling in the car, eating ice cream or a meal, playing a game, walking in the park, putting a puzzle together, painting a wall, going to a museum, riding bikes. Teens want to talk, but don't want the pressure of having to do it without a break.

2. *Avoid distractions.* A safety valve (see #1) is a relief; a distraction grabs attention whether you want it to or not. Is that restaurant a good place to talk, or is the music always too loud? Have you turned off your pager? If you talk in the living room, will you hear little brother bouncing that tennis ball against the garage door? One teen found that even car conversations didn't work in her family: "Sometimes [my parents] are too concentrated on driving or whatever they are doing and don't pay attention to what I am saying."

> "My favorite memories are of my mom and I in the kitchen. Mom was always in the kitchen, cooking or cleaning up. I'd be sitting at the breakfast bar, reading the comics or something, and she would tentatively ask how I was, how my day was, how things were going. Being a teenage jerk, I of course gave her monosyllabic, monotone, 'Yeah' or 'Uh huh' answers, and pretty much blew her off. But she kept trying."
> —A FORMER TEEN

3. *Choose a safe place.* Kids want a place where they feel at ease sharing the scary parts of their hearts. Where is that for your teen? In his room? In yours? On a jogging path? If you don't know, it's okay to ask.

4. *If you find a place that works, stick with it.* Try taking your teen to breakfast or lunch once a week. Establish a habit like this and your kids may get comfortable enough to open up, even asking hard questions about life. Try not to bring your own list of hard questions, though; your teen may begin to shy away from those mealtimes if they turn into interrogations or preaching practice.

Launching Tools

How do you start a conversation with a reluctant teen? Here are six ideas to try.

1. *Talk about a "neutral" issue.* Not every conversation has to be about feelings and relationships. Read a book and discuss the

> "When [our daughters] had a curfew . . . someone was up to greet them when they came home. We might be in bed reading . . . but the rule was . . . come in and say, 'Good night.' The 'trick' behind this was, they knew a parent was going to see them when they came home, give them the 'sniff test,' and the 'talking-to test.' It was also a good time for our daughters to talk if something had upset them."
>
> —A PARENT

choices the characters made. Watch a movie and talk about it (see the *Movie Nights* books from Focus on the Family for ideas). Take an article from a teen magazine and discuss it. Share thoughts about the last sermon the two of you heard.

2. *Use time at the table.* Family dinners encourage conversations, but let everybody share the load. Think of a few questions for people to answer, and avoid judging the replies. Some possible topics: quizzes at school, favorite films, reports due, assemblies attended, geography trivia, headline news.

> *"I love it when I've been going through a rough time and [my parents] just sit me down and say, 'We don't care about anything else. We just want you to know we love you.'"*
>
> —A TEEN

3. *Refine your questions.* Learn to ask gentle questions that require more than a yes-or-no answer. Let's say you and your teen are at a Mexican restaurant. You might start the conversation by asking:

"How is life going for you?"

If your teen just shrugs and bites into that giant burrito, try some less-sweeping queries. "What level of your video game are you at now? What's the most challenging thing about it?"

"How do you think basketball is going? Where do you want to improve? What's Coach Welch say about the team's prospects?"

If your teen still doesn't want to talk about herself, get her talking about her friends. "What do you like best about Sara?"

4. *Make the most of drive time.* Tired of being your teen's chauffeur? Unless talking in the car disturbs your concentration as a driver, discuss topics that come up naturally. That might include the weather, where your teen would like to go if he could

go anywhere, the rudeness of a driver who cuts you off, or the kinds of cars your teen likes.

5. *Use the cover of darkness.* Some kids find it easier to talk at night, especially in the dark. If you go into your teen's room at bedtime to pray, ask for a prayer request; it might lead to his opening up and sharing concerns. Another nighttime opportunity: Greeting your teen after a date, offering a snack and making yourself available for a chat. One parent told us, "We found that if we waited up for them after a date or a night out with friends, they seemed to let down their guard and share more. Some of our best talks happened late at night. And we would have missed them if we'd just hollered out a 'Did you lock the door?' from our bedroom."

Be sure not to turn these post-date wrap-ups into the Spanish Inquisition, though. Debbie Jo and I would start things off with a cheery, "Hey, welcome home! We were just wanting to get a bowl of ice cream with you. Is that okay?" We tried not to stare into their eyes. We'd get that cold stuff on a spoon; right before shoveling it in, we'd ask, "How was it?"

> "My parents were never hesitant to say, 'I love you,' in words and actions. No matter how late I stayed out, they would wait up. Or, they would try to wait up. Sometimes they'd be asleep in their chairs, but the second that door was open, they told me how glad they were that I was home—and we all went to bed."
>
> —A TEEN

Other after-date conversation starters might include, "You looked so great tonight when you went out. Did you feel that way, too?" "I had fun meeting your date. What was he like?" "What was the best part about tonight?"

6. *Try commercial conversations.* Watch a favorite TV show

together and talk during the commercials. View a football game and talk during the halftime show. Watch the news and discuss the stories during the breaks. These short bursts of communication, conducted without having to sit face-to-face, may be just the thing for the really reluctant talker.

Loggerhead Tools

Confrontations happen in practically every home, but they're guaranteed when you and your teen aren't close. How can you communicate in a way that helps you reconnect?

Here are a dozen tips for talking your way through conflict:

1. *Start strong.* Psychologists say the first three minutes of a conversation generally dictate how the rest of it will go. Begin a confrontation with a soft voice and respect for your teen, and it's likely that the confrontation will be more productive and less destructive. As one teen testifies, "My mom and I had effective communication because I was treated as an equal. Not in terms of who was in charge (that was clear) but in that I had a voice."

2. *Let your teen speak first.* Young people we surveyed said that if they have a chance to talk first, they're more receptive to what their parents say. Once teens get to speak their minds, they're usually willing to listen to the other side.

3. *Don't interrupt.* It's tempting to dive in and react to a piece of what your teen just said, but one girl described how that looks from her point of view: "My parents interrupt me and lecture/yell. Then while they're talking and I want to get a word in, I'm yelled at for interrupting. It's really unfair." If either of you tends to talk nonstop, set a timer for two or three minutes and take turns.

4. *Watch your tone of voice and body language.* Model what you want your teen to do. When parents yell or use sarcasm or point fingers, kids figure it's okay for them to do the same. They also put on their protective gear and get into "fight" position. If you turn angry, use a quieter, calmer voice. If nothing else, your teen will have to listen harder to hear you.

5. *Explain what you want and why.* Some teens say they just don't understand what their parents are asking them to do. Have your teen restate what you've told him. Explain the reasons for your request or rule. For example: "I understand you'd like to be with your friends at the concert. But you've been out late every night this week and you can hardly get out of bed in the morning. That's not good for you, or for your schoolwork. Maybe next time."

6. *Fight fair.* No name-calling. Stick to the issue at hand. Don't dredge up past failures. Avoid the words "always" and "never," and don't compare your teen with anyone—living or dead, related or unrelated.

> "Mom was also very good at noticing when something was wrong and leaving me a nice card to show she was there and cared. During one breakup with a girlfriend, I got a letter from the girlfriend, and while I was reading it exclaimed to no one in particular, 'Oh, no!' I didn't talk about it with my parents, but I'm sure it was obvious I was in mourning for this tragic turn of events. The next day I found a card at my place at the breakfast bar that said something to the effect of, 'I'm always here for you,' from my mom."
>
> —A TEEN

7. *Don't beat your teen over the head with Bible verses or biblical concepts.* Sure, it's crucial to pass principles from God's Word on to your child. But most arguments don't qualify as "teachable moments." Your teen won't be too receptive if you declare, "I don't care if it makes you look like a nerd! You'll wear that orange sweater to school because the Bible says to obey your parents. Besides, vanity is a sin!"

8. *Give weight to your teen's feelings and opinions.* You may think it's just "realistic" to tell your teen, "So, the girls said mean things about you. Forget it. You have to get used to people doing that." Instead of feeling like you've just prepared her for the real world, though, your teen will feel dismissed and misunderstood.

9. *Don't try to control your teen's side of the confrontation.* It doesn't work! Let's say your teen is "sassing" you. You could retort, "You will not talk to me like that!" Not a good move, since a statement like this challenges him to prove he, not you, controls his tongue. Instead you could say, "I'll be happy to listen to you when you speak to me more respectfully." Now you're saying what *you* will do—something you *can* control.

10. *Keep the issues in perspective.* How important is this fight, anyway? Is it possible to work toward a win-win solution, or at least one everybody can live with? Are you choosing your battles wisely? Stand up for the values that are most important to you and to your teen's welfare—but consider flexibility on lesser matters.

11. *Take a break when necessary.* If you or your teen are getting too wound up, take a time out. It doesn't hurt to put a conflict on the back burner until people calm down.

12. *When talking fails, write a letter.* Writing gives you time to sort through your thoughts and express yourself carefully. It gives your teen time to respond instead of reacting defensively. A

notebook passed back and forth can work, too; so does e-mail. That's what a mom and dad discovered when their 13-year-old son wanted to see an R-rated movie; they kept telling him no, and he kept arguing. Finally Mom wrote him an e-mail, explaining their reasons. The boy never asked about it again, and seemed warmer toward his parents than he'd been in quite a while.

Take It to the Next Level

Want to close the gap between you and your teen?

Communicating is the key to every relationship, even yours.

No matter where you find yourself on the levels of intimacy, you can build trust between the two of you. You can confront without disconnecting, and in time the confrontations can become fewer and further between. As one teen told us, "[My parents and I] worked on building our communication skills. Now there's less anger and tension between us."

> "Have the hard conversations. Talk about sex and drugs and alcohol without shame or blame. Do your homework; get the facts."
>
> —A PARENT

It's never too late to start communicating with your teen. And it's always too soon to quit trying.

8

Mission: Unavoidable

A boy needs to be validated by his dad. . . . He relates to his dad, and he sees in his father's life what's important to him, and it's usually the dad getting caught up in a job. The need for validation is the need to have a piece of that man's heart and to know . . . that I mean something to this guy. . . . I needed validation that it wasn't something I had to do to earn my dad's love. Validation is a security, and we all need it. . . . Your whole life you're growing up wanting to be like dad, and to know that you are . . . worth something to your father is the most assuring thing that everything is going to be all right. . . . [You may be] great with people and you've got tons of friends, and yet there's just this giant cavity in your heart that was just waiting for your daddy to validate you. . . . The world can't fill it up. A dad's word in a kid's life is critically important, not just something a kid can live without. But your entire life is changed because your dad has validated you.

—A TEEN

I'm going to tell you something now that you may not have heard before. When I first heard it, it blew me away.

It's something family therapist Tim Sanford says:

"It's a dad's role to validate his kids. It's mom's role to nurture."

That might seem to stereotype dads and moms. But Tim explains that validation comes mainly from the father—or at least a male father figure—much as the "alpha male" in a wolf pack determines the place of each member in his family. That's not to say that moms can't validate. It just doesn't seem to be felt as powerfully as when the father does so.

Likewise, nurturing—"pouring life into"—comes mainly from the matriarch of the family. This is most intimately portrayed by a mother nursing her infant. Dads simply can't pour life into a child as powerfully as a mom can. Still, this doesn't negate a father's responsibility to be gentle, kind, and affectionate toward his children.

> "I told [my dad] how my relationship with him has affected my relationship with God. . . . I never saw God the Father as a nurturer or a lover. I just saw Him as a guy who points a finger. And I knew better in my mind, but I had never felt God's love. And I've never felt my dad's love, either."
>
> —A TEEN

What happens when teens don't get the validation and nurturing they need? They look for those things in all the wrong places. That was the case with the young man whose thoughts opened this chapter. Maybe it's the case with your son or daughter, too.

If you're having problems with your teen, a lack of validation or nurturing might be a root reason. The Catch-22 is that the more obnoxious our kids' behavior seems, the harder it is for us moms and dads to even *want* to put our stamp of approval on them.

How can you give your teen what he needs most, even when he doesn't seem to deserve it? That's our project in this chapter.

It's a mission that's not only possible, but absolutely necessary—whether or not we choose to accept it.

What Validation Looks Like

What does "validation" mean? Tim Sanford describes it as words or actions that tell your teen, "You exist, and your existence is good enough. Even when your choices are foolish or your performance is sub-par, you (the human being) are still good enough. You are valued."

Let's say 14-year-old Melissa walks into the living room. Her dad says "Hi, hon." He's validated her by acknowledging her existence.

But what if Dad had a habit of *not* signaling that he knew Melissa had entered the room? It would be like the old "If a tree falls in the woods and there's nobody there to hear it, did it make a noise?" idea. Melissa would assume she's not good enough to warrant a reaction from Dad. She wouldn't be validated.

Anything that says, "You exist and your existence is A-OK," validates your teen. Tim recommends several ways to do that:

1. Attend your child's sporting events or music programs as often as possible. This "proves" she exists; your schedule was altered because of her. The message sent: "You matter to me."

2. Praise your teen after the event for the work he put into it. Explain that you're proud and why. This validates his existence as "good enough"—regardless of the outcome. He thinks, *I'm okay, still.*

3. Be excited (and show it) when your teen gets a scholarship or driver's license or a good grade or a date to the prom. She'll

hear, consciously or not, "I'm excited for you because you're important to me."

You Are Here

Pull into a parking garage, and a machine spits out a ticket. Get your ticket stamped by one of the businesses the garage services, and your parking is free. The store has *validated* your ticket, attesting to the fact that you were shopping there at a certain time.

Validating your teen is like putting your stamp on his psyche. It tells him, "Yes, you are here at this moment."

> "If I did well, we'd go get baseball cards. [But] all I wanted was a dad that I could talk to."
>
> —A TEEN

Why is this such a big deal? Because most of us feel unaccepted, or at least invisible, until someone tells us otherwise. Teenagers, with their self-consciousness and shaky identities, are especially prone to craving this validation. They look for it in friends, parents, stadium and theater audiences, teachers, even online gaming scores. They don't feel okay until someone says in words or actions, "Yes, you exist—and you have value to me."

I had to learn this lesson the hard way. Having been a serious football player and coach, a field that requires strict discipline and analyzing every replayed step, I had a problem with perfectionism. I've also had a critical spirit from day one. I didn't realize this until the day I criticized my son Brady—a sweet, gentle boy—and my wife, Debbie Jo, told me, "Joe, Brady sees himself in your eyes."

Her comment stopped me dead in my tracks. For Brady's first few years I'd been an absent dad; now I was an overly critical one. I'd been assessing my kids, not affirming them.

In time I learned to tell when I'd been overly critical with one of my kids. His countenance would fall, the head and eyes would lower, the body would sag. A parent who loves to be "large and in charge" might take that as a sign of victory; a parent who's looking for relationship knows it's a defeat for both of you.

I'm still fighting my critical, perfectionistic tendencies. But I've worked and prayed to validate my kids. To prove it, my tongue has a blister on it where I've bitten it so many times!

How to Validate Your Teen

How can you validate your son or daughter?

It can be as simple as acknowledging that your teen is in the room. Or saying hello to her when you get home from work. Or using her name when you speak with her.

Or you can get more creative. Validating a 16-year-old son might mean tossing him the family car keys for the evening. For a 15-year-old daughter who likes to cook, it might mean trusting her to choose the menu when your boss comes for dinner.

Ask about your teen's dreams and encourage them. Look at his charcoal drawings; listen to her homegrown band that's been whanging away in the garage.

Find out what music he's listening to, and listen to it yourself—not just to monitor it, but so that you can discuss it intelligently with him. If she's involved in sports, help coach the team. Or at least practice with her, finding out about swim strokes and what makes one stronger and more efficient than another. Go to every game or meet or recital you can. Follow up with positive comments that show you were paying attention.

Don't just applaud performance, though; you're validating the person, not the talent. Focus on character, speaking up when you see inner strength. One father says things like, "I saw you give your last dollar to that lady, son. You have such a generous spirit." Or, "I'm proud of you for making the right decision about helping your sister with her homework."

A lot of kids are starving for that kind of attention. One young man, living in a home for troubled teens, said, "I have never once heard my parents say, 'I'm proud of you.' It's always been, 'You're a smart kid, but. . . .' 'You're a good-lookin' kid, but. . . .'" As that boy told us his story, you could feel his ache to be validated filling the room.

Then there was Jack, whose thoughts opened this chapter. Nothing he did was good enough for his father. Jack was a great baseball player, but his father only mentioned the boy's mistakes on the diamond. Jack says, "There is the need to feel I'm a part of my dad. I needed validation that my successes weren't things I had to do to earn my dad's love."

How to Nurture Your Teen

Validating says you exist. Nurturing says, "Not only do you exist, but I'm going to do what I can to help your heart and spirit thrive."

There's a tenderness to nurturing. I happen to believe that God has given moms especially tender hearts, which suits them perfectly to this job.

If you're a mom, you probably remember a day when your little child came running to you with an index finger held upright, tears running down his face. You didn't hesitate. You took that finger and kissed it to make it better. Your little boy smiled through his tears.

Obviously your teen will have none of that now! So how do you nurture him?

Nurturing, like validation, comes in many forms. Here are three big ones: touch, words, and actions.

Nurturing Touch

Much has been said about how we fail to thrive when nobody touches us. That applies to teens, too—even the ones who glare if we get within a 10-foot radius.

A daily hug is a great place to start. But when you're a teenager, it's not cool to want a hug from your mom. So some moms have declared that *they* need a hug every day. By making it *your* need, you take the pressure off your teen.

Other forms of touch are less intrusive, but still provide nurturing. Try the brush of a hand across an arm, or a pat on the back. Plant a kiss on the cheek or the top of the head while your student is studying or watching television. Daughters often love having their hair braided while the two of you take in a movie on the small screen; one mother said her girls would flop on the sofa and fling their hair onto her lap for her to fiddle with. Sons, meanwhile, will sometimes let their moms massage their heads while viewing TV.

> *"I was probably the most important person in [my son's] life, even though I seemed like the least important."*
>
> —A PARENT

If your teen is truly embarrassed when you're affectionate in front of his friends, wait for a better time. Forcing the issue withdraws from the nurturing bank rather than feeding it.

Be creative as well as appropriate. Ask yourself: How can you show affection without making your teen feel uncomfortable? Try giving your daughter a hand massage; paint her nails. Give your son a gentle punch on the shoulder or tickle those big feet.

Nurturing Words

"Sticks and stones may break my bones, but words will never hurt me." The sad truth is that hurtful words go much deeper than a bruise or a broken bone.

Like the rest of us, teens collect negative words and play them back subconsciously:

"You're stupid and ugly and no one will ever want you."

"You can't do anything right."

"Go away. You're being a nuisance."

"You're just like all the other kids—selfish."

"Come on! Think!"

"[Mom] convinced me that I didn't need to be popular, and [my parents] always encouraged being active in sports while maintaining a femininity. I think that's how I could be described at that time, completely carefree about not being the cool kid, [preferring] to play sports than with stickers or dolls. But at the same time [I] would wear a skirt and have my hair done. These things were influences of my mom."

—A TEEN

Have you heard yourself utter words you wish you could take back? Try words like these that soothe, build up, and encourage:

"I'm so proud you're my daughter."

"Man! You look fabulous today."

"Do you know how much I love you?"

"Want to go shopping with me? I really enjoy your company."

There are so many chances to nuture your teen verbally. You hold the key in your words and tone of voice. And when your teen is hurting, let your voice reflect that pain. Talk softly, asking questions that open your young person's heart.

Nurturing Actions

Here's what one teen who feels nurtured by her mom has to say:

"When I'm going through a tough time, it helps me to cry to my mom. She sits there and gives me a shoulder to cry on and lets me say everything I need to get out. Just knowing she is there to help me out helps me get through tough times. When I finish crying, we talk through what I/we can do to improve/fix the situation."

That mom knows nurturing isn't all talk and touch. Sometimes it's listening.

Sometimes it's doing other things for your teen. For example:

• If it's time to study for finals, bring her hot chocolate or cookies or cut-up fruit in a bowl.

• Do his chores for a day when he's having a bad one.

• Stick you-can-do-it notes on the mirror in her bathroom or bedroom.

• Tuck greeting cards inside his notebook or textbook.

• Text-message a hello.
• Pick her up at school for a surprise lunch at her favorite fast-food place; let her bring a friend if school policies allow.

How Much Is Enough?

Counselor Tim Sanford says children are born with different needs for validation and nurture. Sixteen-year-old Brent may need less validation and more nurturing to feel he's on top of his game. Fourteen-year-old Susie, on the other hand, may need two times as much validation as nurturing.

If you give Brent and Susie equal amounts of validation and nurture, they may feel like they're starving.

Too bad they didn't come into the world with "care instructions" on tags, saying something like, "Jon will need 60 percent validation and 30 percent nurturing. Tumble dry on 'low.'" Since they don't, it's up to you to figure it out. I'm sure God would be delighted to help if you ask.

Observe how your teen responds to validation and nurture. Ask her what she needs more of from you. If she's doing outrageous things—lying to get your attention, for instance—she's probably lacking in one area or the other.

A teen who seems emotionally sluggish might need more nurturing. One who says, "Nobody ever notices me," probably needs validating. A kid who's been labeled a loser by peers, flunked a test, or lost a girlfriend or boyfriend may need both.

> "I don't think [our son's] quest is to know whether or not we love him. It's whether or not we like him."
>
> —A PARENT

Juggling Two Jobs

What about single parents? Can they accomplish this "Mission: Unavoidable"?

Single moms and dads have an extra-tough job when it comes to providing both validation and nurturing. But it's not impossible, as Tim Sanford notes.

In the absence of a father figure, Mom still has power to validate. She can acknowledge her teen, encourage, praise, tell him she's proud of him and his accomplishments. It takes determination, but a single mom can learn how to act more like the "alpha male." She needs to be both mom and dad—for real.

And while validation is most powerful when it comes from Dad, it can be effective coming from another male acting as a father figure. It's important for a single mom to surround her sons and daughters with a few trustworthy men from church, school, family, and elsewhere.

Tim adds that single dads need to make an extra effort to be gentle with their teens. To become more nurturing, don't always try to "fix" problems or people. Listen more and lecture less. Learn from women you trust and respect—and surround your child with them.

I know it's not easy to ask teachers, youth leaders, relatives, and others to help you out by helping your kids. But a conscious effort on your part can pay great dividends.

For those who can't find that kind of support, pick up the task of validating and nurturing as well as you can. Tim Sanford says there's a saying in counseling: "Do what you can, not what you can't." This might be a good motto for single parents. And no beating up on yourself for the things you can't do!

Listen to what one of our Kamp girls said about her single mother:

"My mom spent hundreds of dollars on our traveling sports teams. I cannot remember one game that she wasn't at . . . which is incredible because my brother was in one city and I was in another and she still juggled it all. Her focus was 100 percent on us. Anything we wanted to do, she was involved in. She would take out loans to pay for anything that we wanted to do or try. That was amazing—that she would always make something happen."

That's a heroic mom—one who validated *and* nurtured her teens.

Fill That Reservoir

After I gave a talk to a group of students in one small town, a young lady approached me. The other kids had already told me how they'd tried to entertain themselves, usually getting hurt and heartbroken in the process. But this girl had a lilt in her walk, exuding a confidence the others lacked.

When I asked her about it, she said, "My parents fill my cup of self-esteem so full that my friends can't poke enough holes in it to let all the water out!"

Your teen needs a full reservoir of validation and nurture, too.

You can give your son or daughter a daily supply of both. Through touch, word, and action you can say, "You're here—and I'm glad."

Nothing brings parents and teens together faster.

9

Side by Side

My mom knew how to have fun and make jokes out of stuff, but she knew what was serious and what needed to be taken care of or taken to a higher authority. Because my dad was so strict and anti-fun, we simply learned to avoid him and cut him out of our lives instead of ever respecting his viewpoint or taking his advice.

—A TEEN

The thing that parents must do if they are going to build a relationship and maintain a relationship with their child, is they've got to give up "that dream," whatever the dream is, that the child is not fulfilling. Rather, they have to work with the child to fulfill whatever the child's dream could be, or develop in them a passion or desire to do something. . . . You give them everything you can to help them accomplish all of that. . . . "Whatever you become, I'm going to love you. And whatever you don't become, I'm going to love you."

—A PARENT

An old Ozark Mountain "hillbilly" friend shared some wisdom with my dad a few years ago: "The older I get, the less I know for sure!" That's how I felt when I was raising my teen girls. I couldn't figure out the intricacies of dad-and-daughter psychology. But I worked and prayed and cried over it more than I care to remember!

Don't get me wrong: My daughters were my pride and joy, and I tried every way I could to be the perfect dad. But, man, how many times I failed! I was clumsy and always seemed to be "saying it wrong." I give God and their mom all the credit for the amazing, godly young ladies they were and are today.

During those turbulent and often disillusioning days, all I knew to do was spend time with my girls. Fortunately, that turned out to be the key to the relationship I wanted so badly.

My connecting point with daughter Courtney was on her early morning jogs. She wanted to run three to six miles at 6:15 A.M., so we hit the pavement together. I had to follow her rules, though:

1. We ran at her pace.
2. She did all the talking.
3. I did all the listening.

When I tried to change the pace (a mistake I only made once) or tried to give unsolicited advice (probably more than once), I was quickly corrected and reminded of "the rules."

> *"Sometimes you need to let them do it on their own, rather than helping them so much. My son kind of resented the extra help even though he needed it. He doesn't want me to teach him something in everything that he's doing. I'm learning to shut up. He needs to fix it himself."*
>
> —A PARENT

I still look back on those early morning "joggers" as some of the most important hours I'll ever spend in my life. That's when I learned how vital it is to walk (or run) alongside our teens.

Walking the Walk

We parents of teens are called to leave our paths and get on theirs. Why? To be sure they aren't alone. To encourage them through the thickets and storms. To rejoice when there's something to rejoice about.

When we walk alongside our teens, we usually need to follow their rules. We're there to do what they want to do. We're choosing to actively participate in their world. It might mean joining a neighborhood softball team, or trying out for a community or church theater production, or shooting hoops every night after work, or chaperoning a field trip to a french fry factory.

The fun of doing something together can fill your scrapbook with pages of the best times of these all-too-brief child-raising years. Remember—the days can seem long, but the years are short.

Walking alongside happens when we step into our teens' shoes and see life from their perspective. We don't do it once a year; we do it often.

But where do you begin? How do you walk alongside a kid who may not even like the idea?

Ten Simple Rules

The answer is as unique as your teen's personality and passions. Here are some good ways to discover how to walk alongside your son or daughter.

1. *Find out what he loves to do.* Then do it *with* him, rather than just cheering him on from the stands.

Sometimes what he loves will be obvious, but sometimes it may surprise you both. That was the case with my son Brady, who wanted to be a basketball player. But the pressure of basketball was brutal. I saw potential for something else: music. That didn't come naturally for either Debbie Jo or me; she'd gotten kicked out of choir in sixth grade, and the same happened to me in my junior year of high school.

> "It's so much better when I treat him like a grown-up. It shows love and respect."
>
> —A PARENT

"Brady," I said, "look at those hands of yours. You've got the most beautiful fingers. I can see those on a keyboard. I can see them running up and down the frets of a guitar."

"Well, I'm not interested in music," he replied.

But by the time he was a college freshman, Brady wanted a guitar.

Today he's recording his third album, writing great lyrics and making beautiful music. He sings all over the country; we do youth crusades together. And if you think it's helped our relationship, you're right.

2. *Make the most of summer.* Walking alongside should happen all year, but the best season for growing *with* your teen is summer. Before school lets out, get a calendar and note how many days you have until fall classes begin. Find a block of time *each* day when you can put your priorities, work, hobbies, and worries aside and be there 100 percent for your teen. Plan together what you can do—fishing, camping, shopping, grilling, tennis, whatever your teen would enjoy.

3. *Take a wild adventure together.* Recently my wife, Debbie Jo, took our grandson on a one-day canoe trip down the beautiful Buffalo River in northwest Arkansas. It was gorgeous, safe, and surprisingly inexpensive (canoes rented for just $20 a day). Another family I know hikes in the Rocky Mountains every year.

4. *Ask what your teen has never done but would like to try.* Go try it together. Learn something new. Go with an open mind and a sense of humor—like the lady who, when learning to ski, told everyone that the only rule for the day was to laugh whenever she fell. Look for classes in a foreign language, dance, art, computer software. Take piano or guitar lessons. Sign up for a sports clinic.

5. *Serve the needy together.* Homeless shelters, the Salvation Army, soup kitchens, food banks, convalescent homes, tutoring—the list of volunteer opportunities never gets shorter. One father-son duo did painting and simple repairs at a home for troubled teens, then painted playground equipment for a school in a poor neighborhood. My oldest daughter and I went on a one-week mission trip to Trinidad when she was 13, and it was the best thing we've ever done together. We found common goals, common ground, and made memories that helped us through the most difficult years of our relationship.

> *"Walk alongside their dreams, not changing them to your own."*
> —A PARENT

6. *Find out what your teen dreads doing.* Ask whether she wants your help with that PowerPoint project about bacteria or that awkward phone call to a friend whose sister just passed away. What kind of assistance does she want? Remember to follow her rules—for example, letting her be the boss about where things go when you help clean her room.

7. *Walk alongside your teen spiritually.* At Kamp Kanakuk our

counselors have devotions with the kids, once and sometimes twice a day. In Kamp K-2 football, we pray each day with 40 rugged teen guys before or after workouts and memorize a Bible verse together. It connects me to the kids and connects the kids to God. You can make the same kind of connection by praying and reading and memorizing Scripture with your teen daily.

Just 10 minutes a day can give your relationship an "eternal touch." School may get what's in the middle, but I was determined to "bookend" my kids' days with a short devotion at the breakfast table and a Bible-and-prayer time before bed.

Three of my four kids really liked our twice-daily times together. I never forced my kids to be part of them; we only had those times when I was welcome. For the uninterested teen, I was like an old, faithful dog—ready in the corner, but not pushy. This old dog didn't jump on the reluctant child every time she came through the door, saying, "Let's talk, let's have a devotional." I was just available.

This should be "sanctuary time," a safe place in today's uncertain world. Don't use it for lecturing, criticism, or manipulating

> "We've communicated to him that we love him. We've done it in every way possible. We've told him we love him, we've demonstrated our love for him. We've gotten to the point now where he clearly understands that we love him unconditionally, that we will work with him to help him accomplish whatever dreams he will have."
>
> —A PARENT

"My parents have always been awesome encouragers. They support me in all areas of my life, and I really feel loved because of that. They're definitely my biggest fans/encouragers. . . . They've been there through the good and the bad. And even though I know I hurt them sometimes, they're still there for me 100 percent."
—A TEEN

your teen with God's Word. With those ground rules, your teen can look forward to spending time with you.

My advice is to ditch the word "devotional," too. It's not Sunday school; it's your set-apart time, your quiet time, your sanctuary.

8. *Bring your teen into your world.* When I ran errands, I'd invite one of my teens to come along. If I was speaking at a youth rally, there was a place for my kids on the team coordinating the event. When my teens came home from a party or a date, I invited them to "debrief" over a bowl of cereal with me.

9. *Discover your teen's dreams.* There's a dream inside every young person, as sure as there's a yolk inside every chicken's egg. Help your teen identify his strengths and work together toward realizing his dream. My book *Wired by God* (Focus on the Family, 2004) is one tool that can help you do that. Guide your teen in setting his own goals; then investigate ways for him to gain skill and experience.

In our family, Courtney enjoyed gymnastics and volleyball; Brady was into guitar and basketball; Cooper liked weight training and football; Jamie pursued cheerleading. I was the lucky guy who got to catch passes, spot flips, and cheer like crazy. Listening

to saxophone practice and retrieving tens of thousands of basketball shots helped build foundations for friendships with my kids
that I enjoy as an "old
guy" today.

> "Hug your kid often. Meet their friends. Encourage your kid to form real relationships with quality people. Encourage them to shine. Encourage them to find their strengths and then play to them. Your kid is not you. Let your kid shine in his or her own way."
>
> —A PARENT

10. *Remember that the relationship is every-thing.* During those crazy teen years, my relationship with my kids was top priority. The media were telling them to have fun through sex, drugs, and alcohol; peers were telling them that parents were no longer relevant. I wanted to earn a hearing by being
the person my kids loved hanging out with the most.

No matter how you decide to walk alongside your teen,
remember that it's not a chore. It's not a competition, either. The
goal is to learn about your teen, to have fun, to encourage, to do
some servant-hearted foot-washing.

Walking alongside your teen takes time. It may even start out
as hard work. But before you know it, the process will be a joy—
because you'll really enjoy this person you're coming to know.

Success Stories

If you're still not sure whether it's worth it to walk alongside your
teen, listen to these young people brag on their parents:

> My mom was there for me by being my biggest cheer-
> leader. She could always tell if I was down or up . . . and

she always knew what was going on. If I said I didn't want to talk at that moment, she respected the boundary and knew I would talk when I wanted to. If I had a big test, I would tell her, and she would help me study. She knew what was happening and was genuinely interested. She even tried to listen to my music sometimes, to connect with me and have fun. She went to all my color guard competitions and helped with the booster club to fundraise. She left little notes for me all the time as an encouragement. And she prayed for me, all the time.

I can't remember a single choir concert or school program where both my parents were not in attendance. They volunteered with youth group functions at church. They let me know that our house was always open for my friends and I to come hang out. And when my friends and I did go to my house (which was frequent), Mom and Dad quietly disappeared and let us have some fun (after they said hello and offered Cokes and snacks and whatnot). When I had something to say, and not just something deep, but a random remark about my day, Mom or Dad would immediately mute the TV or turn off the radio and ask me a question about it, or just make eye contact and let me know that they were listening. In fact, my parents asked a lot of questions, and I told them things that I probably wouldn't have mentioned otherwise. When I was excited about something, they were excited with me. (My mom would even dance around the kitchen!) And I still love to tell my mom great news because she gets so excited.

When my prom date dumped me a week before prom, [my parents] were righteously indignant, and Dad offered to pay for the whole thing if I could find a date that fast. All in all, they were active, involved parts of my life—not just the people who paid for my food and shelter. They truly were parents to me.

They have been with me every step of the way, always knowing what was going on in my life, and still are. Now that does not mean that I never had a chance to become independent; that's not the case at all. They definitely let me go out with my friends and basically do what I wanted—within limits—because we had developed a level of trust in our relationships. I had earned that freedom and independence when I was pretty young.

My parents were always interested in what was going on in our lives, what we were up to, who our friends were. They came to and supported all that we did. They encouraged us in certain areas of our life and discouraged us in other areas.

My mom did walk alongside me. . . . As I was going through something teens deal with, like friend issues, she would lend an empathetic ear and not judge the situation, or tell me, "It'll all be better in a few years." She trusted me enough to make my own decisions and helped me without making me feel powerless.

There you have it, from the experts.

Show me a parent who walks alongside his teen, and I'll show you a teen who's likely to finish the race well. That teen may wander off the track; she may stumble; she may fall. But she'll have the preparation to be able to get back up, dust herself off, and run until she hits the finish line.

"As my brother and I got older [our parents] definitely started to back off, letting us start to make our own decisions and develop our own opinions on things. . . . This past fall my parents at different times sat down with me and discussed important issues that come with being an adult soon to be on my own. They are preparing themselves and me . . . [for] 'walking alongside' us. They know that it is time for me to definitely have figured out my own reasons and beliefs for the things I do and don't do. All this does not mean, however, that my parents won't still be there for me. They are still going to be concerned with what's going on in my life, and I will want to tell them!"

—A TEEN

Surviving the Detours

In my mind, I rationalized and I justified that doing drugs and hanging out with guys 20 years old was okay because I had that resentment toward my parents. So, it's okay for me to do these drugs, because there's a lot going on in my life. I manipulated it to where it pleased me. That's my whole life . . . all my life I've been a manipulator. I'm a thousand different people in one, because I can pretend like—I pretend like I'm your best friend, and that's only just to be getting something from you. . . . I cry every night before I go to sleep.

—A TEEN

Every day I receive letters and e-mail from Kamp Kanakuk parents who are broken, bruised, and filled with questions. Why have their kids rebelled? What did the parents do wrong? When will the fighting and worry and shame end?

I've empathized with every story. And if I've learned anything from these parents' pain, it's that formulas don't work. Nothing "works" in the sense of being guaranteed.

You can "come home." You can apologize for being gone, and for anything else that may have contributed to your child's anger and distance. You can promise to listen better and cheer your teen on and walk alongside him. Some kids will observe for a while and see if you really mean it. If you do, they may come back and let you into their lives again. But others will continue on their detours, lured into the dark places by their own determination or by the lies of the enemy.

They're commonly called prodigals. If you have one, this chapter is for you. If you don't, read it anyway—because you probably know parents whose teens are giving them this kind of grief, and who need your understanding and support.

Parents of Prodigals

The worst nightmare of many Christian parents is to have a prodigal—a kid who makes her own destructive way through life, ignoring everything she's been taught, refusing to abide by any rules, causing chaos in the lives she touches. The fear is so great that some parents stress over everything their teens do, taking even normal behavior as a sure sign that their kids are headed for the edge of the cliff.

> "It's so hard when you're doing everything you can and you don't see anything working."
>
> —A PARENT

Other parents do the opposite. They ignore obvious warning signs, hoping it's all a phase their kids will pull through. I've talked with moms and dads who couldn't believe the alarms they missed—a pot-smoking son coming home glassy-eyed and wanting to devour every snack in the house, an alcoholic daughter returning on weekend nights and vomiting on the front lawn.

Remember Sandra and Richard McDonald from Chapter 1,

who discovered their son Kurt had helped a friend break into a truck? Later they would say, "We didn't think our son was capable of anything like that. Now we're finding out, okay, he's done some serious drugs, he's been involved in a crime, he's hanging with a kid we hate. That night started us on the process of determining what we should do with him because it was apparent we had a problem here that was bigger than we were."

No parent wants to live through something like this. But more and more are being forced to these days. They're finding that no matter what they did to raise their children "right," it's possible that one or more will rebel.

Tough Love

This is a tough chapter to write. Tough because I can't be there to put my arm around you, pray with you, and encourage you. Tough because there's no easy answer to your situation. Each kid is different, and will take his own detours.

That's why each situation needs to be assessed individually.

> "[Our son] didn't care what happened. That's why he would take the risks he was taking. He'd just gotten to that point where he really didn't care what happened, saying, 'I wanted to see what it was like, and I just didn't really care whether I lived or died or what happened.'"
>
> —A PARENT

Consulting a pastor or counselor is wise; sometimes more drastic measures need to be taken. When a teen is a threat to himself or others, for example, a place where well-trained professionals can monitor him 24 hours a day may be the best call. There are many good Christian counselors and programs available.

> "[Our son said,] 'Get me some place to go because I hate being with you.' When we left him [at the residential facility], as we left, we said, 'I love you.' He said, 'Well, I hate you.'"
>
> —A PARENT

The temptation is to walk away, to throw up your hands and surrender. You wouldn't be alone if you did. Many parents want to give up—and do. Unable to take the pain any longer, they protect themselves by pretending it doesn't matter. Accepting their child's "Leave me alone!" they remove themselves emotionally from his life.

What these folks don't realize is that even though the teen's every action and word are designed to push the parents away, deep inside he longs for a mommy and daddy to hang tough, to keep trying—to be there for him no matter what.

You Need Help

Should you arrange an intervention for your alcoholic son? Should you bail that shoplifting daughter out of jail? Does your son's Attention Deficit Hyperactivity Disorder explain his skipping school? Would telling your daughter not to see that boy with all the body piercings help or hurt?

Your pastor or counselor is the one to talk to about handling your particular prodigal. Your plan of action must be tailored to your situation, and chances are it will require long-term, in-person guidance. What I want to do is help *you* get through this process.

I'll start with two principles I've learned through my own parenting.

1. *God is not on vacation.* He's not oblivious to what you're going through. Nowadays my kids are grown and we're all best friends, but it wasn't always that way. During their growing years there were plenty of incidents that just about caused me to double over in pain. At those times I had to remind myself that the God who sees sparrows fall sees our frustrations, too.

2. *Don't carry what isn't yours to carry.* If you tend to be a little controlling—as I do—this can be a tough one. But ignoring it leads to burnout and bitterness.

It boils down to this: Today let God have what's His and keep only what's yours. As my wise father used to say, "Work like it all depends on you, but pray like it all depends on God." Your teen's future and safety and ability to walk through trials are in God's hands. So is revenge for the hurt you've been dealt.

> "We needed to get him out of that situation and get him help. Be humble enough to realize right then someone else can do a better job than you."
>
> —A PARENT

Jesus said, "For my yoke is easy and my burden is light" (Matthew 11:30). If you're hauling luggage around right now that isn't yours to haul, give it to the One who carries it well.

Principles from Prodigals' Parents

It's one thing for me to tell you what I've learned. What about parents who've watched their kids "choose stupid," who've been dragged down the most dangerous detours, who've agonized and cried and prayed and made seemingly impossible choices—yet somehow survived?

I've talked with moms and dads like these, and want to share their insights with you. It's surprising how many of them report learning similar things about what it takes to make it through. Here are some of their hard-won observations.

1. *You can't control your teen's choices.* Once your daughter leaves the house, there's no telling what she's doing. She can listen or not listen in class. She can throw out the good lunch you made and eat grease-laden fries covered with nacho cheese and suck down a 64-ounce Coke. She can take drugs, cheat on tests, drive drunk— or study hard and land in the top 10 percent of her class. She can be class president or class clown. And there's nothing you can do about it.

2. *God allows all of us to make poor decisions.* Generally speaking, God doesn't step in to rescue us when we pick the wrong path. If we decide to have sex with someone other than our spouse, He doesn't lock the two of us in separate rooms. If we choose to blow through a stop sign because we're in a hurry, He doesn't stamp His foot on the brake. If we wait too long to get those tires replaced, He doesn't drive the car by remote control to the nearest Firestone dealer. He teaches us, but He usually doesn't undo our choices. He lets us learn from running too fast over the rocks and falling and skinning our knees.

"I just wanted to say, 'Forget it. Just let her go her own way.'"

—A PARENT

3. *Allow your teen to face the consequences of his choices.* One parent said, "It's really difficult to know when to step in and when to allow God to let life teach the lessons."

Some moms and dads refuse to believe their little Bobby could cheat on a test, or that Susie would ever write such trash about someone else and pass it around (though it's obviously her handwriting). These parents swoop in to rescue their children. If Ginger gets a traffic ticket, Dad's right there to pay for it. If Josh missed three football practices, Dad will hound the coach to let Josh play.

What does this teach Josh and Ginger? That there are no consequences for poor choices. That someone will always rescue you. That there's no need to take responsibility for your own actions, because there's always someone else to blame. But if God feels it's important for us to learn through the consequences of our choices, why are we shielding our kids from the consequences of theirs?

4. *Learn the art of relinquishment.* This means letting go. It may mean releasing your dream for who your child would be, giving up control over your teen, leaving the results to God. One mom, Barbara Ryan, wrote this description of relinquishment:

What does it mean?

It means to let go with one's hands but not with one's heart.

It means to stop striving to control that which will not be controlled.

It means the end of ceaseless worry and anxiety and the dawn of entrustment which leads to peace.

It means giving back to God that which He has given you with the humble admission that you need divine help.

It means anticipating bad news while still praying for good news.

It means a deeper walk, and a moment by moment seeking of wisdom to discern when to render aid, and when to withhold it.

It means holding before oneself and the wayward one a picture of what is sought, what the reasonable expectations are, while calmly barring the door to manipulation, unacceptable compromise, and lesser standards.

It means scanning the horizon for hopeful signs, yet not pursuing the prodigal.

It means continuing to tend one's flock, and to plow one's fields, to the best of one's ability.

It means continuous intercessory prayer that the Creator would have mercy on His lost sheep and that He would pursue that sheep in your place and stead.

"I just grabbed onto anything . . . anything that was positive."

—A PARENT

It means the humility to stand before men, acknowledging that you are a miserable sinner (capable of making mistakes) who nevertheless did the best he could given the light revealed in prior times of decision, and maintaining internal peace even if judged or misunderstood.

It means a moment by moment willingness to share with others who are also scanning the horizon for their prodigal.

It means a quiet confidence that every ounce of travail will be met with consolation, both now and in eternity.

It means pressing on to know the Lord, while maintaining faith, love, and humility.[1]

5. *Get help for yourself and your family.* If you broke your arm, you'd rush to the emergency room for help. So why are so many moms and dads ashamed to get help when a family is broken?

Some folks prefer pastoral counseling; others opt for a therapist. Just be sure the advice is well-founded in Scripture and in a knowledge of adolescents. It would be foolish to take that broken arm to a dentist, and foolish to take your family to someone who doesn't understand teens or the One who made them.

6. *If necessary, get your troubled teen out of the house to protect the rest of the family.* When a teen becomes violent or brings home illegal activities like drug-dealing, it's time to act on behalf of your family's safety.

Forcing your teen to live elsewhere is no easy decision, and should be made with the concurring wisdom of a professional. But if your teen is unmanageable, don't hesitate to find a residential facility where he has a chance to turn his life around. At the very least, it's a place for him to be relatively safe until he's 18 and can sign himself out to live where he wishes.

"All your emotions are going nuts because you're so desperate. You're scared, you're angry. Crying. Not knowing what to do. There's really nobody to help you, but God. And, well, He's invisible."

—A PARENT

For help in locating a program or residential facility that might suit your situation, talk with a Christian therapist in your area—or call the counseling department at Focus on the Family (1-800-A-FAMILY).

7. *Don't be afraid to let others know what you're dealing with.* One parent admitted, "We didn't want the whole world knowing [about our prodigal teen] because my husband was an elder in the church."

You don't need to share details with gossipmongers, but be real. Many parents have been surprised at how God used their transparency to help families in similar situations. Pain shared is lessened; shared joy is increased. As another parent of a prodigal recalled, "It became apparent that the Lord wasn't dragging us through this as an isolated adventure, but that it turned into a ministry opportunity. And it took us a while to get excited about that, but it really didn't take very long."

8. *Ask for prayer.* Don't be shy. Tell those you trust that your teen is making poor choices with her life, and you'd love for them to pray. Find one or two to be prayer partners and ask them to pray for you daily.

9. *Pray.* Go to God with everything. Don't be afraid to express every emotion. If you're desperate, tell Him so. If you're angry with Him for not keeping your kid corralled, let Him know. But give Him a chance to speak to your heart, too.

If you have other children, pray as a family. In the words of one parent, "I feel like God's hand was definitely in all of this, all through the whole process we've been through, putting us where we belong—which was on our knees or prostrate on the floor, praying, " 'Help. We need help. What do we do?' "

Don't know what to pray? I love this prayer that Karilee Hayden wrote about her wandering daughter, Wendi:

> Dear Lord,
>   Merciful and loving Savior, again I bring my heart's greatest longing to You. Wendi continues to run from You. She continues to make poor choices. She is getting entangled so deeply in her sinful ways . . . I don't even know if she's gone beyond hope. But I ask for Your mercy upon her and

our grandkids. Father, I pray that your Holy Spirit will break through her heart of stone. Almighty God, I ask that You draw her to Yourself. I commit her into Your keeping—again—for this day, even though she is so far from You. Please deliver her from the evil one, I pray. Amen."[2]

10. *Don't look for good, look for God.* Some well-meaning people say, "Look for good in the situation." You know what? Sometimes there's no earthly good to be seen. Sometimes there is only God.

Author Sandy Lynam Clough writes, "It is a waste of time for us to frantically look for good in a bad situation. What really helps is to look for God. Sometimes we can't see His hand working, nor can we force His hand. We need to be looking for His face, because it is His very character that will keep us in peace until the 'good' is manifest."[3]

> "Sometimes the best things come out of the hardest things."
> —A PARENT

Look for God in Scripture. On index cards, write verses that are especially meaningful to you and put them where you'll see them. Write your own psalms in a blank book, expressing yourself honestly as David did.

Look for God in hymns and worship songs. One prodigal's parent said, "I had one really godly friend. She didn't really care if I called her three times a day, and she would say, 'Read a psalm, go sing a hymn.' This friend would also say, 'God is the Redeemer and He is in the business of redeeming. He didn't bring this about to not bring redemption out of it. . . .You've gone through so much. He's not going to let go of you now.'"

Look for God at work in everyday life. In a notebook, write down "small" things you believe He's doing. Refer to it when things look bleakest.

Trust that God has not abandoned you even if you don't sense His presence. He *hasn't* abandoned you. After hearing the stories of hundreds of kids and parents who've endured major detours, I'm more convinced than ever that "neither death nor life, neither angels nor demons, neither the present nor the future, nor any powers, neither height nor depth, nor anything else in all creation, will be able to separate us from the love of God that is in Christ Jesus our Lord" (Romans 8:38-39).

11. *Praise God.* I'm not going to tell you to thank God for your child's wandering. How could any loving parent gladly watch his child destroy herself? Instead, we praise God not *for* the chaos but in the *middle* of it. We praise Him for being perfect, for being our Creator, for His holiness, for His love—for the same reasons we've always praised Him. We also praise Him for being there for our teen, even when we can't be.

12. *Take care of the rest of your family.* The teen in crisis usually gets the attention. Make sure that your marriage (if you're married) and your other kids (if you have some) aren't ignored.

> "We're not to blame. We aren't perfect, but we did the best job we could. God, the rest is up to You."
> —A PARENT

One parent said, "Strengthening our marriage made us much more able to deal with the issues at hand." Another observed, "It's like any trauma in life—it forces you to live in dependence upon God. What it does to a couple is extreme. There is no middle ground. It either forces them into a deeper relationship with each other, or it forces them apart. We are closer as a result of all this. That is something I can say I'm thankful for."

As for your other children, they need you more than ever. Don't be surprised if they misbehave for attention themselves, or try to act like angels for the same reason. Some kids, on the other hand, withdraw and try to care for themselves so that the stressed-out parent doesn't have to.

13. *Allow yourself some enjoyment.* Many couples who have prodigals put themselves in suspended animation, grimly hanging on "until this thing is resolved." Some feel guilty about having fun when they should be "doing something" about the problem, or too vigilant, tense, worried, or embarrassed to enjoy anything. But you can't keep going without recharging.

Don't neglect the physical side of your relationship with your spouse. Take a weekend off. Set a regular date night and don't talk about the kids during that time. Relax in a bubble bath. Rent a funny movie and watch it together.

14. *Hold on to your core values.* Don't let the continuing attack wear you down. Did you believe before that God knows your situation, right down to the number of hairs on your head? He still does. Have you always felt it was important to give your child a present on her birthday? It still is. Did you think you needed to use your gift of encouragement in the children's ministry at church? You still do.

15. *Try writing in a journal.* Recording your thoughts, feelings, and prayers can help you sort through the garbage and discover what's important. You can use a notebook, a blank book, or a computer. You could even e-mail your entries to a trusted friend.

16. *Be relentless.* It's never giving up. It's moving forward no matter what. It's not stopping the good stuff. It's trying new things when old things aren't working. It's sticking with the things you know are right. It's loving unconditionally. It's staying put as a parent when you'd rather run. It's being with our teens the way God is with us.

Karilee and Dan Hayden know the meaning of the word. For over 10 years their daughter Wendi took a long and winding detour, making the most destructive choices along the way. But they hung in there—praying for her, loving her, never giving up. Wendi, like the prodigal son in Jesus' parable, finally came around.

17. *Be tough and tender.* You need a thick skin and a sensitive heart. That's especially true when it comes to dealing with the comments of others. Karilee Hayden recalls, "Several times onlookers approached Dan or me with platitudes such as, 'Perhaps God is going to let Wendi wallow in the pigpen for a while,' or well-intentioned comments as to how some children 'just have to learn the hard way,' and so on. These comments, though perhaps true, were of no comfort to me personally. I wanted love. I wanted understanding. I wanted hope—and I wanted nothing more than to have others join with me in prayer for my beloved daughter."[4]

Even well-meaning people can be hurtful. Don't let their barbs penetrate, but be tender enough to hear the supportive words others may offer.

> "The worst possible circumstances can have the best possible result, and that's God."
>
> —A PARENT

18. *Don't try to play God.* Karilee Hayden struggled with wanting to help the Holy Spirit along. She arranged situations that she thought would "fix" Wendi.

"I hoped her brother's presence at home would whet her appetite for things of the Lord. Perhaps Rob, a vibrant Christian young man with a strong sense of leadership and love for others, would draw her into spiritual things. Perhaps his Christian friends, often hanging out at our house, would have a positive influence on her. Perhaps the warmth and love of our church body would soften her heart. Perhaps . . . perhaps . . . perhaps. . . ."

Karilee's hopes usually were dashed. Finally she realized she'd been building on sand, figuring out a "solution" and telling God how to carry it out. "What was wrong was my attitude of self-control, and putting my hopes in a preconceived and self-concocted result instead of the person of Jesus Christ. It was good and right to bring my hopes, dreams and requests to God (in fact it is a Scriptural command—Philippians 4:6,7). But my hope had been anchored to my own plan and not upon God Himself and in His sovereign and perfect plan for Wendi and me."[5]

You can't be the Holy Spirit. You can only be a parent who's relentlessly loving—and leaving the results in God's hands.

Those are the lessons learned by moms and dads who've been there.

I can only add one truth that hit me a few years ago, when I was being treated for leukemia. When the world seemed most empty, God's love filled my heart. When the future seemed most uncertain, the hugs I got from Him were the most reassuring.

It was then that I saw how real a promise can be: "Can a mother forget the baby at her breast and have no compassion on the child she has borne? Though she may forget, I will not forget you! See, I have engraved you on the palms of my hands; your walls are ever before me" (Isaiah 49:15-16).

He won't forget you, either—or your teen.

Too Soon to Quit

Teenage kids are chemical- and testosterone
(or estrogen)-laden animals. Do everything you can
to understand how they feel and cut them some slack
for acting stupid. Do everything you can not to be
waylaid by all the junk that comes up when dealing with
a teenager. Remember your mutual purpose . . . or
reinvent one together, and stick to it.

—A PARENT

Mom, thank you for not giving up on me. Thank you
that I know that you're always there for me.

—A TEEN

When the tsunami rolled over Banda Aceh, Indonesia, on December 26, 2004, truck driver Mustafa Kamal was far from home. He returned to find his wife, three daughters, and brother had vanished.

Kamal stubbornly refused to believe his little girl, five-year-old Rina Augustina, was dead. Haunted by visions of her, the anguished father searched everywhere. He went from street to street, building to building, day after day.

On January 25, 2005 the Associated Press reported the result of Kamal's month-long search. A powerful, moving photograph documents the moment that father and daughter were reunited, thanks to the efforts of the Save the Children organization. When Rina spotted her daddy, she ran into his arms.

Kamal screamed, "By the grace of God! I knew you were alive! I knew it!" Then he added, "My precious little one. I did not give up. I kept looking."[1]

That dad was relentless.

He never gave up, never stopped hoping, never quit.

What better picture of a relentless father than Mustafa Kamal, searching single-mindedly for the daughter he loved so much?

How about the picture provided by our relentless God, who continues to pursue us despite the grief we give Him?

Relentlessness: Finishing the Job

One parent of a teen said, "I felt like I failed so bad. But the Lord gave that relentless love to me, that love that just would go by [my

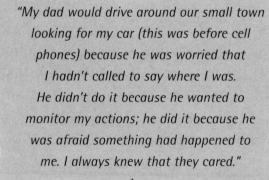

"My dad would drive around our small town looking for my car (this was before cell phones) because he was worried that I hadn't called to say where I was. He didn't do it because he wanted to monitor my actions; he did it because he was afraid something had happened to me. I always knew that they cared."

—A TEEN

son's] bed and pray over his bed at night and be there for him at
two in the morning when he was drunk. I remember him letting
me pray for him, right then."

Whether your teen is in a
"far country" or just slightly off
the track, it's not easy being a
relentless parent. It can be
mind-numbing to take your
kid to Saturday breakfast week
after week, only to hear endless complaints about a sister
who "keeps taking my stuff." It can be painful to see the latest "F"
on a report card, and to hear your repeated offer to hire a math
tutor rebuffed. It can be heartbreaking to get still another phone
call from still another policeman in the middle of the night.

> *"My parents trusted me com-
> pletely, as long as I was honest
> with them. But if I broke the
> trust and stayed out too late, or
> hid something from them, they
> let me know instantly."*
> —A TEEN

But the payoff is worth it.

What will your payoff be? It might the moment when, at one
of those boring breakfasts, your son asks how you chose your
mate. Or what is most important to you. And listens to your
response.

It might come when your daughter finally agrees to enter
rehab. Or moves out of a live-in relationship. Or asks what time
church starts, in case she decides to show up after all.

God doesn't guarantee U-turns. But He makes them possible,
and uses our efforts when it pleases Him to do so. And scriptures
like these hold out hope for every relentless parent: "Being confident of this, that he who began a good work in you will carry it
on to completion until the day of Christ Jesus" (Philippians 1:6).

God wants you to join Him in finishing the task of raising
your teen. That may feel like an unrunnable marathon sometimes.

But keep your eye on the finish line! Even if you have to stagger or crawl, resolve never to give up.

Daily Diligence

My years with four teenagers in the house were definitely the toughest of my life. My heart broke into a million pieces as I shared my kids' many pains during those wild and turbulent times.

It set me to praying—every day. I asked God to make those six teenage years golden years. I prayed that my kids would have godly hearts. I prayed for their sexual purity, for their ability to stand alone against peer pressure, for their self-images, for their desire to honor and obey us, for wisdom, for their friends and teammates and teachers and coaches and future mates. I prayed that the example of my life would be more consistently godly.

> "I know we did not do everything the best we could do, but we did the best we could do at the time. It wasn't always excellent and it wasn't always the greatest, but it was the best that we were capable of at that moment."
>
> —A PARENT

I made many mistakes with my kids, but I didn't quit. I tried to be diligent in doing what I thought was right, adjusting my tactics with each situation and each kid, and adjusting again when my methods didn't work.

In the process, I discovered some tips you might find useful. They're the kind of thing you might be tempted to forget in the heat of the parenting moment—the kind of thing that takes daily diligence.

1. *Allow choices whenever possible.* When we're rushed, or when our teens have disappointed us, it's easy to step in and make the decisions ourselves. But kids learn to make good choices . . . by making choices. If good choices lead to pleasant results and poor choices produce painful consequences (which they often will if you don't "rescue" your teen), you'll probably find your son or daughter making more of the former than the latter.

> "[You need to tell your teen,] 'I'm sorry, but here's the result of that behavior.' Don't always make it an authoritative battle on who's in charge, but stick with your consequences and stay calm."
>
> —A PARENT

2. *Remember the power of saying, "No."* It's part of a parent's job, so don't be timid! "Everybody" may be doing it, going to it, watching it, listening to it, drinking it, and using it, but "In this home, we're not!" Don't just issue declarations, though; keep working on the relationship and explain the reasons behind the boundaries.

3. *Follow through with appropriate consequences.* If your teen comes home before curfew, praise her. If she ignores the limits you've set, withdraw an allowance or privilege (driving, phone use, going out at night, etc.). In the interest of fairness, let your teen know ahead of time what the limits and penalties are. For example, coming home 15 minutes late means coming home 15 minutes early next time. Write it down so no one forgets!

George Callahan is one dad who discovered the value of appropriate consequences. He and his daughter Miriam spent way too much time bashing heads—especially over getting the girl to school on time. Finally George decided to lay out what he was going to do: "The car is leaving for work at 7:30 A.M. If you're ready, I'll take you to school." If Miriam wasn't ready for school then, she had to find another way to get there.

George says, "It changed everything to just get out of the power struggle and say, 'We don't have to struggle. I simply present the consequences. Those aren't negotiable.'"

4. *Re-evaluate your habits occasionally.* Every so often, honestly assess where you are and how you're doing as a parent. Give yourself credit in the areas where you're doing well, and thank God for His help. In other areas, create a simple, step-by-step plan for improvement. Be firm with yourself, but not harsh.

> *"I do lose faith. I do lose the desire to go on all the time. I'm always losing it."*
> —A PARENT

5. *Be consistent.* Some parents find this the toughest task of all. But teens like to know where they stand and what's expected of them. When rules change and they get in trouble, they withdraw or lash out. Some families find it helps to draw up agreements, even in the small things, so there's no confusion about what's expected.

One teen boy said, "I've never had a set curfew. One night it will be 12 and the next night, even if I haven't done anything wrong, they'll be like, 'Oh, come home at 11 tonight.' It was very confusing."

6. *Be patient.* Give yourself—and your teen—a break. You're going through a time of upheaval and delicate wire-walking. Allow yourself some slack when it comes to measuring progress.

One wise parent puts it this way: "We had to take on a different perspective and realize that all things weren't going to be fixed or worked out. There would still be conflicts. That relationship didn't have to suddenly be right for us to be happy or content."

7. *Keep up with your teen's world.* Even in the midst of chaos—or

because of it—you need to know about the culture that's pressuring and misinforming your son or daughter. Subscribe to magazines like Focus on the Family's *Plugged In*. Set your Internet browser to http://cpyu.org/, The Center for Parent/Youth Understanding.

8. *Enjoy your teen*. Being a parent to a teen is not all hard work. There can be a lot of fun, too. Teens are daring, willing to play and explore life; they're often enthused, outrageous, crazy, insightful. They can be great companions when you're running a quick errand. Think of your teen as a new friend you'd really like to get to know. Try not to lose sight of that, even when you don't think you could love this kid one more second.

> *"I just kept believing that God really was going to do what He promised and redeem the situation."*
>
> —A PARENT

9. *Meet apparent rejection with acceptance*. "No matter how sullen they were, we hugged them," one parent said of her teens. "[We] said we loved them. It didn't matter if they responded. We did it anyway. Now there isn't a conversation that doesn't end with, 'Love you, Mom!' 'Love you, Dad!' They open their arms and hug freely."

10. *Make encouragement a habit*. One teen says his mother posts a new Bible verse every day on his mirror. This young man is honest enough to say he doesn't always read them. But he loves that his mom is consistent and caring enough to do it, even though she knows he doesn't always read them. Her diligence shouts love to him.

It's Not Over Yet

Your teen is still growing, changing. The story isn't finished.

You're in Act Two, where there's a new twist in the screenplay.

It's a critical point, a catalyst for upheaval—but it's only one step on the way to resolution.

It's too early to give up. You're in the middle of a job, the middle of a game, the middle of major surgery. It may look as though all is lost, but that's only because you can't see the ending.

This is the critical part of your journey with your teen. It's the part where your teen learns that you love him no matter what. And that God does, too.

> "These are the kids who are going to be the warriors for God, because once they get on the right track . . . there is nothing that's going to stop them."
>
> —A PARENT

That was the case with Stephen and Carissa Sheldon, whose son took a rebel's road. "Faith is that . . . sense of assurance that God's got this thing in hand and . . . a peace that you walk through the day with," Stephen says. "I did not have that. I do have faithfulness, however, and that's pure, dogged, stupid persistence. I'm committed to hanging in there with my son. I'm committed to the process, and I'm committed to working my way toward [him]."

When things looked darkest for their son, the Sheldons realized that, as Stephen puts it, "God really does love that boy." He adds, "I think that became one of those defining moments that carried us through the rest of it. I guess I still hold that in our mind right now, and it's just ground out in prayer. . . . There are so many times we were just ready to pack it in, surrender, and say, 'Forget it, I've lost it, I've lost all interest, I'm surrendering on this, I give up.' But I guess we continued to [remind ourselves], 'God really does love us. . . . God really does love that boy.'"

The Gain of Pain

There's another reason not to give up: You and your teen may actually benefit from the struggle you're going through.

No one likes pain. But a relentless parent allows pain to do its work when he knows it will teach that son or daughter hard truths about life. A relentless parent also lets his teen see him wade through pain with God's help.

Here's how parent-of-a-prodigal Karilee Hayden puts it:

> I knew that God reaches out in love and tender provision to His children in time of need; but I had to come to grips with the fact that sometimes God's plan includes pain and heartache. Sometimes it includes waiting. Sometimes His answer is no. That is how He fulfills His many-faceted purpose in our lives. That is how He "grows" us. That is how we become conformed to His image. And that is how we become beautiful vessels to be used to His honor and glory. I needed to allow God complete and unquestioning control, looking to Him alone, and not the result I had envisioned.[2]

It's tough sometimes to believe that pain can help. But as one wise parent reminded us, a teen's detours might be compared with the way Jacob wrestled with God (Genesis 32):

> God ended the wrestling match by crippling him. Jacob probably went through the rest of his life . . . taking very, very painful steps. But each one of those steps was a

reminder of his reliance and his dependence upon God.
And I guess for us, we're crippled. I've got a limp in my life
that I will never, never be cured from. But I would like to
think that the crippling effect has in fact served as a beautiful reminder each and every day that we have to live in
dependence upon God.

I believe that a 16-year-old or a 21-year-old that is in
the process of developing his limp is a good thing, but it is
so hard as a parent to watch that process take place.

Moms and dads naturally want to jump in and fix things
when the pain starts. But fixing is God's job. Listen to this wisdom from a mom:

I think before, our daughter felt that we were trying to fix
her and that she was the only one in the family that
needed fixing. What I've learned is that, when kids are at
[a residential program for struggling teens], they don't get
fixed.

We all need fixing, and God showed us things that
needed fixing while she was gone—and so now our relationship isn't based on trying to get her fixed. Because I've
seen how much God has worked in her life, I trust Him a
whole lot more and know that He is the One, He is the
only One, who can change anything in her. So, I think
having that pressure off of her mom trying to fix her all the
time has made our relationship better.

Can you trust that God is working in your teen whether you
see it or not? Can you believe that pain may be part of that process?

God can purify our kids—and us—in the fires of trial (1 Peter 1:7). When you doubt that, look back on how He's used pain to refine your own character.

When Will It Be Over?

Is there a time when you can quit trying?

No.

Even though the door slams one too many times. Even though the purse is emptied of cash—again. Even though you think your heart can't take it anymore.

Why not quit? Besides the reasons I've already named, there's always the possibility that your teen—perhaps even as an adult—will wake up and want to come home.

> "Being apart really made [our daughter] realize that her home situation was probably not near as bad as she imagined."
>
> —A PARENT

No, there are no guarantees. But it's happened in countless cases. Parents of distant or rebellious teens sometimes talk about a "catalyst moment" when their kids suddenly realized what they were doing. It was as though a dark room became flooded with a light that left no shadow. Catalysts can take many forms, most of them unexpected by moms and dads.

Some kids' detours are relatively short. One teen, tired of being the "good girl" and assuming her parents loved her only because she behaved all the time, grew a rebellious streak the width of a football field. Her folks kept loving her, drawing boundaries, and letting her suffer the consequences of her actions. After a year she was back, confiding to her parents that she was testing them—seeing whether they loved her for what she did or for who she was.

Other kids' detours seem to last forever. I heard recently of one lady who prayed for the salvation of her daughter's friend. The friend finally did receive Christ—after the lady prayed faithfully for 50 years!

Let me give you permission to give up on your kids—when God does. He won't, as one mom testifies:

> God doesn't take His hands off of our kids. Now I know He heard me even when I felt like I was doing everything I could do, and praying, and not knowing if He heard because I couldn't see any answers. But now I can see that when we don't give up and we keep taking it one day at a time and we keep giving it to the Lord, giving [my son] to the Lord and letting go, things can happen. There may not be things that I see in my lifetime that God's going to do, but I know I've got to keep praying.
>
> Something that keeps encouraging me is seen all the time—that when we can't see the sun through the clouds, it's still there. Just like God and His work in my son's life.

When You Get Discouraged

Maybe your biggest hope for your teen is summed up in 3 John 4: "I have no greater joy than to hear that my children are walking in the truth." And maybe you've seen that hope dashed time and again.

What can loving, relentless moms and dads do when that happens?

1. *Look for small signs of progress.* Don't expect a daughter who hates doing chores to become Molly Housemaid; settle for paper

plates in the garbage instead of on the floor. When your home-work-hating son takes enough responsibility that you only have to check up on him twice an evening instead of four times, be glad.

2. *Find an accountability partner besides your spouse.* Choose an honest person who sees you with your teen. If you struggle with frustration that flares into anger, tell your accountability partner and have him check up on you. Your partner should also be an encourager, cheering you on when you feel you can't finish the marathon.

3. *Count your blessings daily.* Even if the bills are unpaid and your teen hasn't spoken to you in 72 hours, the blessings of God are endless. He loves us and gave His Son for us. He provides wisdom for parenting, though not always in the way we might expect. Try listing your blessings in a journal, aiming not to repeat the same ones too often. Remember the hard times and ask God to show you how He blessed you then.

> *"God is certainly capable of completing the work that He's started—even though it took us a while to believe that He's still at work."*
>
> —A PARENT

4. *Pray.* Throwing yourself honestly in God's lap day after day changes your life. Honest prayer says, "I don't feel like forgiving that kid for being sassy one more time. Can You help me?" It says, "I have no idea what I should do about Rachel's grades dropping. Will You show me?"

In my own home, before Debbie Jo and I crash on the pillow at night we get to read a chapter in the Bible and pray together for our kids. Lately we've been reading about God's man, Samuel. God honored the prayers of Samuel's mom, Hannah, as she dedicated the boy to the Lord. He also honored her efforts to raise a godly man, using Samuel to unite Israel and bring David into leadership for the greatest days of that nation's life. God will hear your prayers for your son or daughter, too—and honor your work as a loving, relentless parent.

It's in Their Hands—and His

According to counselor Tim Sanford, the only thing that will bring a prodigal home is "coming to his senses" and beginning to make wise, healthy choices. It's common for parents to feel guilty over something they think they should have done or not done—as if that will make the differ-ence and bring their way-ward son or daughter home. But a parent can't make a prodigal turn out "right." God is in control, but we're not.

> *"I've seen God work, and that's the greatest encouragement to see your prayers answered. When you pray you don't really think God's going to answer them. And when He does, you go, 'Oh, my goodness! He answered it!'"*
>
> —A PARENT

Nevertheless, there are some things parents can do as part of "tough love" with a minor who's still in their custody. An appoint-ment with a school counselor or professional therapist is often the place to begin; sometimes a teen will hear words from another adult that she won't hear from her parents.

There are times when a teenager's behavior makes it necessary to remove him from the home and place him in a residential treat-ment center. Parents are often reluctant to do this, believing it means giving up on their teen or having failed as a parent. Not true! And as Tim Sanford observes, it's better to seek outside help earlier rather than later.

What if your teen gets in trouble with the law? It's hard for many parents to allow the legal system to step in and take its toll. But don't stand in the way. Don't run lickety-split down to the courthouse to bail your teen out. If he earned the consequence, let him receive it. That may be the beginning of his realizing the effect of his foolish choices—and the beginning of change.

A parent may choose any of these action steps in hopes of encouraging a teen to reconsider her present path. But as Tim reminds us, prodigals return home when *they* come to their senses and start making better choices.

That was the case with a young man we'll call Randy Anderson.

His mom began having problems with Randy when he was 13. She was a career naval officer; she and her two sons moved a lot. After one of their moves Randy began ditching school, stealing from other students, vandalizing, and lying.

They'd attended a good church. But Randy, now as tall as his mom, refused to get in the car on Sunday morning. Mrs. Anderson sought help from the youth pastor and school counselor, but Randy wouldn't cooperate with anybody.

> "You know, there's no advice I can give other parents. It's just holding on."
> —A PARENT

When Randy was 16, his anger and rebellion reached a new level: He physically threatened his mom. She dialed 911, and the police took Randy out of the home. By the weekend he was placed in a residential treatment center.

Randy was assigned to a male caseworker. The two of them worked on issues of abandonment, grief, and anger during his six-month stay. Finally Randy received a deferred sentence for the most recent vandalism charge and was told to keep his "nose clean" until he turned 18.

Moving back home, he attended the required number of therapy sessions. With the court watching over his shoulder, he attended all his classes—but refused to do any homework.

The vandalizing and physical threats stopped. But Randy began experimenting with alcohol and bullied his mom and younger brother every chance he got. Blaming all his problems on Mom because she "sent him away," he refused to get a job or do any chores. He also found ways to take money from his mother without being caught.

Mrs. Anderson stuck with the "tough love" approach, continuing to set and enforce boundaries even when it seemed harsh and uncaring. Randy badgered her relentlessly for his driver's license, but she refused. She also declined to be his private taxi whenever he demanded to be taken somewhere. She kept praying and had a couple of close friends who kept praying, too. She saw a therapist from time to time to be sure she was on the right track.

"[What keeps you going is] just your commitment to the Word and your commitment to the commitments in the Word."

—A PARENT

When Randy turned 18, Mrs. Anderson told him to leave the home. It was the hardest decision she'd ever made. She cried for days, even though she knew it wasn't safe to have her son there anymore. His anger was out of control.

The young man left. He stole a carton of blank checks from a neighbor's mailbox, ending up in jail for fraud. When he called his mom demanding she post the $2,000 bail, she refused. Randy was furious.

After nine months in jail, he was released on parole. His

parole officer took a special interest in him and tried to help the young man learn to make smarter decisions.

To the surprise of everyone who knew him, Randy decided he needed some discipline and structure in his life—and joined the Army. After basic training he met some Christian soldiers and a great chaplain. He started attending chapel services. Slowly he began making wiser decisions.

> *"You never quit. We went on for five years before we turned the corner. . . . We lived a day at a time. Sometimes a minute at a time."*
>
> —A PARENT

In time—after a total of 10 years of tears, prayers, sleepless nights, and holding firm to her boundaries—Mrs. Anderson got a phone call from her son. He wanted to apologize.

Things still aren't "happily ever after" for the two of them. But they've reconciled and are working on developing a healthy relationship. Randy still harasses his mom sometimes—whenever Army beats Navy. But it's only in good fun now.

As Randy's story shows, even though there are no guarantees that prodigals will return, there is hope.

Things Change

Don't forget that parenting has its seasons, and seasons change—often for the better.

One season that lasted for a long time in our family involved my eldest daughter, Jamie. She'd always been Daddy's little girl—until something happened in seventh grade that neither she nor I understood.

It seemed to begin the day Jamie and her younger sister,

Courtney, were riding in the pickup truck with me. Feeling very good as a dad, I was about to tear my shoulder muscles from patting myself on the back. "Hasn't this been a great year?" I asked. "Haven't we had a great year as father and daughters?"

My enthusiasm clashed with the silence in the truck. Both girls stared straight ahead. Finally, fifth-grade Courtney, queen of integrity, said, "Jamie doesn't like you very much."

I was stunned. Looking past Courtney, I saw Jamie hugging the truck door. "Really?" I said. "Tell me about it."

Jamie replied, "I haven't liked you since November."

It was March.

"Can you help me understand that?" I asked.

A torrent of frustration poured out of her. "My friends go to movies that you won't let me see. My friends wear clothes and jewelry that you won't let me wear. They get to pierce and you won't let me. My friends go to parties you don't let me go to. And I don't like you."

> "I guess I just feel like the things that I had hoped for that I couldn't see—I can see them now. I remember that scripture phrase, 'Now faith is the substance of things hoped for.' And I remember back then, you know, I just had to hope for that. And now I'm seeing it in his life."
>
> —A PARENT

Wow. I had no idea.

Thinking fast, I kept my eyes on the road and my grip on the wheel.

"That makes me sad," I told her. "But you know what? That's okay. I *want* to be your friend, but my *job* is to be your dad. If you don't like me until you're 23, that's okay.

"But when you're 23 or 25 or whenever," I continued, "then you're going to be in the back of a little chapel, slipping on a white gown and a white veil. Peanut, you are going to be the most gorgeous bride, just like your mom. And I'm going to walk you down the aisle. At the front of the aisle will be the best man you've ever met. He'll take a bullet for you. You'll be the love of a lifetime for him. When you walk down that aisle you won't be ashamed. You won't have regrets.

"My job is to make sure that as you walk down the aisle, you have no regrets. And when I place your hand in his, then take my seat in the front pew, I want you to be able to turn around and say, 'I like my dad.' If you don't like me until then, that's okay."

She didn't say a word.

Months passed.

On another day, this time in the car, she turned to me again. "I bought you a present," she announced.

"What is it?" I asked.

She slipped a CD into the player. From the speakers came the song "Wind Beneath My Wings." On the chorus the car rang with her message:

"Have I ever told you you're my hero?"

She still struggled with my authority. But I knew that in her heart, I was her hero.

> "[It's great] just seeing him being self-motivated and not having to push him to do an assignment. . . . Just getting involved in sports again, going on dates, just all the things you want to see your kid doing in high school. All the fun things. He [isn't] in that darkness anymore. He [has] new friends."
>
> —A PARENT

Giving me that present didn't end her dislike of me. We both worked at our relationship, but it was hard.

Then came the day when, after she was married and became pregnant with her first child, she approached me in tears. "Daddy," she said, "I don't know why I'm so mean to you."

"I don't know, either," I said.

I held her, both of us crying.

We're best friends today.

There's a mystery in the teen-parent relationship. It's beyond fathoming. Somehow, with time and God's help, things change. And in this case, the changes are very likely to be improvements.

The Finish Line

I'm at the finish line, cheering you on. But as much as I'm here for you, God is here so much more. He loves you, and He loves your teen.

Love isn't simple, though, and it's not easy. This parent knows that from experience:

We think love looks like buying stuff for our kids, looks like keeping them at home until they are way too old to be at home. And you know, that's not love.

And we had to totally redefine what love looked like for [our son] Peter— love that makes him the person God meant him to be. And for us, that meant kicking him out of our house when he was 17 and risking him going on the street. But we knew that was love.

That looked like hate. That looked like disdain. But it

was love—because it was what brought him to the point of saying, "I need help." And he never would have gotten there if we'd continued to rescue, to provide, to just sort of be that soft landing for him. And a lot of these kids, they have to get the hard landing before they sort of get it.

As you let your teen take the "hard landings" of life, remember that God is there to teach, train, and grow her character.

Don't give up on Him.

Don't give up on the power of His relentless love—or yours.

Even at your lowest points, you can do as this mom did: "I looked my daughter right in the eyes and I said, 'You know, Anne, I promise you this: I am never going to . . .' And I know she was expecting me to say something terrible to her. I said, ' . . . I am never going to give up on you.'"

> *"I mean, it's over-whelming that he would hug me and tell me he loves me."*
> —A PARENT

That mom also says, "Anne could rise to be that wonderful young lady that I think God fashioned her for. We're just not quite there yet."

Sooner or later, I believe they will be.

Notes

Chapter 10

1. Barbara Ryan, "Relinquishment," unpublished essay. Copyright © 1999 by the author. Used with permission.
2. Karilee Hayden, *Wild Child, Waiting Mom: Finding Hope in the Midst of Heartache* (Carol Stream, Ill.: Focus on the Family/Tyndale House Publishers, 2006).
3. Sandy Lynam Clough, *And I Know He Watches Me* (Eugene, Ore.: Harvest House Publishers, 1999), p. 55.
4. Hayden, *Wild Child, Waiting Mom.*
5. Ibid.

Chapter 11

1. "Five-Year-Old Girl Found After a Month," Associated Press, January 25, 2005, found at www.msnbc.msn.com/id/6862983.
2. Hayden, *Wild Child, Waiting Mom.*

FOCUS ON THE FAMILY®

Welcome to the family!

Whether you purchased this book, borrowed it, or received it as a gift, we're glad you're reading it. It's just one of the many helpful, encouraging, and biblically based resources produced by Focus on the Family for people in all stages of life.

Focus began in 1977 with the vision of one man, Dr. James Dobson, a licensed psychologist and author of numerous best-selling books on marriage, parenting, and family. Alarmed by the societal, political, and economic pressures that were threatening the existence of the American family, Dr. Dobson founded Focus on the Family with one employee and a once-a-week radio broadcast aired on 36 stations.

Now an international organization reaching millions of people daily, Focus on the Family is dedicated to preserving values and strengthening and encouraging families through the life-changing message of Jesus Christ.

Focus on the Family Magazines

These faith-building, character-developing publications address the interests, issues, concerns, and challenges faced by every member of your family from preschool through the senior years.

| Focus on the Family **Citizen®** U.S. news issues | Focus on the Family **Clubhouse Jr.™** Ages 4 to 8 | Focus on the Family **Clubhouse™** Ages 8 to 12 | **Breakaway®** Teen guys | **Brio®** Teen girls 12 to 16 | **Brio & Beyond®** Teen girls 16 to 19 | **Plugged In®** Reviews movies, music, TV |

More Great Resources
from Focus on the Family®

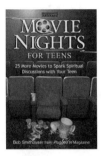

MOVIE NIGHTS FOR TEENS-
In this sequel to the popular original book, 25 chosen movies are examined with a range of themes and story lines—to spark interesting conversations with their plots, engaging questions, Scripture applications and more. From recent releases to vintage gems, *Movie Nights for Teens* brings families together to discuss movies, culture and wise entertainment choices.

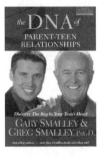

THE DNA OF PARENT-TEEN RELATIONSHIPS
Conflict is an inevitable part of any home with a teenager. Gary Smalley and his son Greg use family stories to illustrate the incredible difference honoring one another makes—especially during a disagreement. Plan now to forge lasting bonds using the honor principle.

WIRED BY GOD
Your teenagers probably have a million dreams for the future. *Wired by God* shows you how to identify the desires in their hearts and start turning them into reality. Filled with fun, interesting ways to pinpoint gifts, talents, personality traits and more, this unique set will spark great conversations that will bring you and your teen closer.

Includes a free teen workbook on CD-ROM with expanded self-assessments and planning tools for teens to use on their own.

FOR MORE INFORMATION

Online:
Log on to www.family.org
In Canada, log on to www.focusonthefamily.ca.

Phone:
Call toll free: (800) A-FAMILY
In Canada, call toll free: (800) 661-9800.

BP06XP1